The Essential Nisargadatta

Edited by Roy Melvyn

The Essential Nisargadatta

Edited by Roy Melvyn

Copyright 2013 Roy Melvyn

First paperback Edition September 2014

Summa Iru Publishing

Boulder, Colorado 80020

Contents

Who is Nisargadatta Maharaj?   6

The Nectar of His Teaching   9

Core Instruction   11

Full Instruction   23

Written Words of Nisargadatta   201

Atmajnana and Paramatmayoga, "Self-Knowledge and Self-Realization"   202

Spiritual Knowledge and the Pacification of the Desire to Know   225

Tying It All Together   228

"There is no sense of personality at all when you become the Ishwara principle. Have no concern about losing your personality by listening to this knowledge, as personality has always been illusory. In order to even understand me the sense of personality must be absent.

You are the knowledge and you don't have any shape or form whatsoever. You are impersonal. You are comprehensive. You are the unmanifest, the Universal Consciousness. What would happen if you went in search of that Consciousness? The seeker would disappear in the search, because the "I Amness" is all there is."

Nisargadatta Maharaj

Who is Nisargadatta Maharaj?

When asked for details about his birth and early life, Maharaj would say "I was never born" or "Why to talk of things that have not taken place!". I suspect that was his way of drawing attention away from what he deemed utterly unimportant.

On another occasion, this one an auspicious birthday celebration in his honor, he declared to the assembled in the Laxmibaug Hall of Bombay:

"Today's celebrations are not in the glorification of any individual. This is an auspicious occasion for you and for me to glorify the unity of a devotee with his Satguru [fully enlightened Guru established in Reality]. To name a particular day as being the birthday of One who is not only eternally existent but eternal existence itself is, in the spiritual parlance, incorrect. It is also wrong to personify a true devotee. As long as you conceive yourself to be an individual male or a female being you will not be the all-pervading, eternal and transcendental Self. Go with the conviction that you are not the bodily self, that you are beyond births and deaths, that you are dynamic, being dynamism itself and are apparently experienced only as pure and simple awareness. Be free, proclaim saints, go on asserting within that Self [one's true nature] is not weak or devoid of power. Believe steadfastly with a simple belief that Atma is rich with its fullness. It is not possible to delve deep enough to reach the seed – the Gurubeej – the inner faith on Satguru. Devotion to Guru reaches the Guru through devotion to the Self and the Satguru's blessings emerge and flower through the Self and are consciously received externally by the devotee. Godhead is nothing but pure awareness of your being. The achievement of this fruit – this Godhead – is accomplished through unshakeable faith in the pure Self. That is what is called the satswarup, the Self, is through this faith thoroughly comprehended. There should be conviction of this comprehension. The conviction implies unshakeability. That should be accomplished. There should be unflinching conviction of the Self being fixed, immobile. That which you conceive yourself to be is myth because you take yourself to be the bodily being. The incomprehensible on the surface of which the awareness of being is experienced is called the Satguru. Call conviction only to that which does not budge, which is immobile. Supreme Reality is fixed, immobile. The Self is fixed in supreme Reality. The Self is supreme Reality."

However, humans seem to love narrative, so in the spirit of compromise, I will offer a brief biographical sketch to my reader.

Nisargadatta Maharaj was born in March 1897, on the day of the birthday of Lord Hanuman in Bombay and was brought up in a village named Kandalgaon in the lovely countryside, 4 to 5 miles deep from Malwan, a seaport to the south of this District. In keeping with the local custom, being born on the auspicious birth anniversary day of Sri Maruti, Maharaj was named Maruti.

Maharaj had his elementary education up to Standard. IV at Kandalgaon.

Maharaj left for Bombay in 1918 to explore life there. He occasionally would go to Kandalgaon to look after the land there. He had endeared himself there to all with his obliging and friendly nature. Even in those olden days he had befriended many harijans. He had at times even helped them drag carcasses. His pure mind did not even so much as think of inequality amongst men.

After intermittently being either in Bombay or in Kandalgaon for two to three years, Maharaj permanently settled in Bombay in 1920. He joined a night school for a short while and acquired the rudiments of English. He worked for a couple of months as a clerk in the Princess Dock. The constraints of service inhibited his enterprising mind. He therefore left his job and entered business.

Owing to his industrious and friendly nature, his business prospered. The scale of his business slowly started enlarging. Shops, big and small, of tobacco, beedis [hand-rolled cigarettes], cutlery, ready-made garments, etc., were opened by him at Khetwadi, Grant Road and Bori Bunder. Although he was making good money, but he had not forgotten his devotion to God.

He married in 1924.

A friend pressed Maharaj to have darshan of Sri Siddharameshwar Maharaj, but he avoided it. However, his friend would not let up and eventually Maharaj agreed to go and listen, and subsequently sought initiation. Siddharameshwar Maharaj by disclosing one secret thing, created confidence in him and initiated him by giving a Nama Mantra and explained to him how to meditate. Within a few minutes Maharaj experienced dazzling illumination of various colors and went into deep trance. Siddharameshwar Maharaj soon thereafter awakened him.

The conviction in Sri Siddharameshwar Maharaj's teachings transformed Maharaj's life. His zest for family life and business waned. He practiced meditation and sang devotional songs with sincerity.

Siddharameshwar Maharaj died just before the Divali festival in 1936. Maharaj was haunted by his words: "Disciples as such there are many, but is there one who is ready to renounce material life completely for the sake of his Satguru's word?" It tormented his mind. He became completely distracted; his business was soon neglected.

A year later, he renounced the material world and began to wander. Only after many months, did he finally return.

He found his old business in ruin and he could retain only his present beedi shop in Bombay. During this time, he began talking with friends who were moved by the depth of his understanding. Over time, the few increased in number.

Requests for initiation ensued, which Maharaj consistently rejected. However, by 1951, he yielded and started, in deference to the will of his Satguru, to initiate true aspirants by giving them Nama Mantra.

In this fashion, he assumed the role of a guru.

The Nectar of His Teaching

(Editor's Note: The contents of this book are derived from audio and written transcripts of talks Nisargadatta gave in his loft from the late-60s until his death).

Although the scope of Nisargadatta's teaching is truly vast, at its root, it can be said to revolve around a single question: What is our true identity?

His answer is: In unmanifested, stillness, our identity is the Absolute Unicity, Pure Awareness not aware of itself; manifested, functioning in duality, our identity is consciousness seeking itself.

He declares that one's true nature is ever-free awareness, as the source of, but distinct from, individual consciousness. It is only the I-am-this-body idea that keeps us from living from our "original essence", our Self.

It is an essence that is pure, free, and unaffected by anything that occurs. It watches all events with impartiality. All that exists is the total functioning of the Absolute Reality operating through the infinite forms in manifestation.

He argues that the interconnectedness of varying forces in the universe is so vast, that everything depends on everything else and that singular events, in and of themselves, are acausal.

On our original state of the timeless, changeless, Absolute Noumenality, the body and mind have appeared uncaused as part of the total functioning of the Impersonal Consciousness. Each phenomenal form acts during its allotted time and at the end of its life, it disappears as spontaneously as it appeared. Then consciousness, merges in Awareness. One is neither born nor dies. Only forms come and go. The psychosomatic complex acts in accordance with its nature, and we are the witness of the actions. We are timeless being as the source of both life and consciousness.

The most commonly used word is the word 'I'. To delve into the sense of 'I' in order to reach its source is all he talks about. Discontinuous, this 'I' must have a source from which it flows and to which it returns and this is what he calls the self-nature. The gateway to the one reality, is this sense of 'I am'. When one goes beyond it to its source, one can realize the supreme state, which is also the primordial.

Core Instruction

Along with the knowledge 'I am' appears space and the world. When the knowledge 'I am' departs the world is liquidated.

Appearance and disappearance, birth and death these are qualities of 'I am', they do not belong to you, the Absolute.

Catch hold of the knowledge 'I am' in meditation and the realization will occur that 'I', the Absolute, am not the quality 'I am'.

Do nothing but stay in the knowledge 'I am', the 'moolmaya' or primary illusion, and then it will release its stranglehold on you and get lost.

Establish yourself firmly in the 'I am' and reject all that does not go with it.

Forget all about physical disciplines in this connection and just be with the knowledge 'I am'. When you are established in the 'I am' there are no thoughts or words.

Get stabilized in the primary concept 'I am' in order to lose it and be free from all concepts. In understanding the unreality of 'I am' you are totally free from it.

Apply your mind, go back in time and try to recollect the moment when for the first time it dawned on you that 'you are' or 'I am'. This nascent 'I am' is without words or non-verbal.

By meditating on the knowledge 'I am' it gradually settles down at its source and disappears, then you are the Absolute.

Catch hold of the 'I am' and all obstacles will evaporate, you will be beyond the realm of body-mind.

Go on to know the 'I am' without words, you must be that and not deviate from it for even a moment, and then it will disappear.

Go to the 'I am' state, remain there, merge, and go beyond. If you were to dwell in the 'I am' and firmly abide in it, all external things will lose their grip on you.

Having acquired and understood the knowledge 'I am' stay there in seclusion and don't wander around here and there. Once you stabilize in the 'I am', you will realize that it is not the eternal state, but 'you' are eternal and ancient.

Hold on to the 'I am' very firmly, ever abide in it and it'll dissolve, then you are as you are.

You have to realize that you are not the body or the knowledge 'I am'. You as the Absolute are neither, nor do you require them.

You have to transcend the 'I am' to enter the concept-free Parabrahman state, where you do not even know you are!

You must meditate on the 'I am' without holding on to the body-mind, the 'I am' is the first ignorance, persist on it and you will go beyond it.

You should identify yourself only with this indwelling knowledge 'I am'. That is all. Sit in meditation by identifying with the 'I am', dwell only on the 'I am'- not merely the words 'I am'.

Your Guru, your God is the 'I am', with its coming came duality and all activity, stay on the 'I am', you are before the 'I am' appeared.

Immortality is freedom from the feeling 'I am', to have that freedom remain in the sense 'I am'.

In deep meditation, infused only with the knowledge 'I am', it will be intuitively revealed to you as to how this 'I amness' came to be. It is prior to the 'I am', it's the unborn state, so how can it have or even require the knowledge 'I am'?

It is the 'I am' that investigates the 'I am' and on realizing its falsehood it disappears and merges into eternity.

Just sit and know that 'you are' the 'I am' without words, nothing else has to be done; shortly you will arrive to your natural Absolute state.

Keep focused on the 'I am' till you become a witness to it, then you stand apart, you have reached the highest.

My Guru taught me what 'I am', I pondered only on that. My original state is to be in that state where there is no 'I am'.

What is it in you that understands this knowledge 'I am' without a name, title or word? Sink in that innermost center and witness the knowledge 'I am'.

When the 'I am' goes all that remains is the Absolute, give all your attention to the 'I am'.

When this concept 'I am' departs there will be no memory left that 'I was' and 'I had' those experiences, the very memory will be erased.

When you meditate on the knowledge 'I am', which is the beginning of knowledge, how can there be any questions? It is not with the body identification that you should sit for meditation. It is the knowledge 'I am' that is meditating on itself.

When you remain in the 'I am' you will realize everything else is useless, and then you are Parabrahman, the Absolute.

With the arrival of the primary concept 'I am', time began, with its departure time will end; you the Absolute are not the primary concept 'I am'.

Witnessing happens to the state prior to your saying the words 'I am'. Right now, right here, you are.

You are neither the 'I am' nor its activities, you as the Absolute are none of these. Be a true devotee, by abiding in the knowledge 'I am' thereby transcending the experience of death to attain immortality.

You are the Reality beyond the 'I am', you are the 'Parabrahma'. Meditate on this and remember this, finally this idea, too, shall leave you. Understand the 'I am', transcend it and realize the Absolute.

This sense of 'being' or the feeling 'I am', was it not the very first event or happening before any of your living experiences could begin?

To do away with body-mind sense or identity, imbibe or dwell in the 'I am'. Later the 'I am' will merge into the ultimate nature.

Totally accept the knowledge 'I am' as oneself, and with full conviction and faith firmly believe in the dictum 'I am that by which I know I am'.

Understand that the knowledge 'I am' has dawned on you and all are its manifestations, in this understanding you realize you are not the 'I am'.

Understanding the 'I am', your sense of 'being' or just 'presence' is extremely important as on it rests the entire outcome of the teaching.

You have 'to be' before anything else can be, your sense of 'presence' or the feeling 'I am' is really fundamental to anything that has to follow.

One who has realized the knowledge 'I am', which means transcending it as well, for him there is no birth or death nor any karma.

Only the 'I am' is certain, it's impersonal, all knowledge stems from it, it's the root, hold on to it and let all else go.

Out of the nothingness, the 'I am' or beingness has come, there is no individual, the knowledge 'I am'- not the individual – has to go back to its source.

Putting aside everything, stabilize in the 'I am'. As you continue with this practice, in the process you will transcend the 'I am'.

The One who abides in that principle by which he knows 'I am' knows all and does not require anything.

The teaching is simple, when the 'I am' arises, everything appears, when 'I am' subsides everything disappears. Onto your Absoluteness, which is without form or shape, came this knowledge 'I am', which is also without shape and form.

The very core of this consciousness is the quality 'I am', there is no personality or individual there, reside there and transcend it.

This 'I am' is still there with you, ever present, ever available, it was and still is the first thought, refuse all other thoughts and come back there and stay there.

This knowledge 'I am' has spontaneously 'appeared' on your Absolute state, therefore it is an illusion. The feeling 'I am' is itself an illusion, therefore whatever is seen through this illusion cannot be real.

Remain focused on the 'I am' till it goes into oblivion, then the eternal is, the Absolute is, Parabrahman is.

Remember the knowledge 'I am' only and give up the rest, staying in the 'I am' you will realize that it is unreal.

Sitting quietly, being one with the knowledge 'I am', you will lose all concern with the world, then the 'I am' will also go, leaving you as the Absolute.

The 'I am' has great potency, the entire manifestation has come from it. When you dwell in the 'I am' as your destiny you realize that your destiny is not death but the disappearance of 'I am'.

The 'I am' in body form can reach the highest state only if you understand, accept it and dwell there. Then you escape birth and death.

The 'I am' is the sum total of all that you perceive, it's time-bound, the 'I am' itself is an illusion, you are not the 'I am' you are prior to it.

The beginning and the end of knowledge is the 'I am', be attentive to the 'I am', once you understand it, you are apart from it.

The body identity cannot get this knowledge, the knowledge 'I am' must get this knowledge; when knowledge abides in knowledge there is transcendence of knowledge.

Full Instruction

While I am talking about it ('I am') I take you to the source of the spring. There, water is coming out in a trickle now. This trickle subsequently becomes a river, an estuary, and finally the sea, I take you to the source again and again. Once you arrive at the source, you come to know that actually there is no water, the water is purely the taste, the news that 'I am'.

You have to give up everything to know that you need nothing, not even your body. Your needs are unreal and your efforts are meaningless. You imagine that your possessions protect you. In reality they make you vulnerable. Realize yourself as away from all that can be pointed at as "this" or "that". You are un-reachable by any sensory experience or verbal construction.

You have to go within. Whatever great things have happened in nature, however powerful, still they disappear right here. These situations appear and disappear. This is actually abstract, what is solid here is the knowledge 'I am'. The seen and seeing, disappear. I tell this only to those who are prepared to listen. Whatever appears is bound to disappear.

You have to realize that you are not the body or the knowledge 'I am'. You as the Absolute are neither, nor do you require them.

You have to stabilize in your present true nature, 'I am'. All other secondary and redundant objects should be got rid of. Do not focus you attention on any of these things. The whole process is to be in your source. At present, what is your source? 'I am'. Catch hold of that 'I amness' and be in it. You have to realize your own self. You must be at the borderline between 'I am' and 'Not-'I am'.

You live in the house but the house is not yourself. Similarly the knowledge 'I am' is in the body, but it is not the body. When the knowledge 'I am' is not there do you perceive or observe anything? Knowingness is knowledge and no-knowingness is also knowledge, but it has no form. Call that knowledge 'I am' as your Self; don't call the body as knowledge. The knowledge 'I am' is the primary God, meditate on that only.

You may know all the right words, quote the scriptures, be brilliant in your discussions and yet remain a bag of bones. Or you may be inconspicuous and humble, an insignificant person altogether, yet glowing with loving kindness and deep wisdom.

Beyond the mind there is no such thing as experience. Experience is a dual state. You cannot talk of reality as an experience. Once this is understood, you will no longer look for being and becoming as separate and opposite. In reality they are one and separable, like roots and branches of the same tree. Both can only exist in the light of consciousness, which again arises in the wake of the sense 'I am'. This is the primary fact. If you miss it you miss all.

First of all, this knowingness appeared, the knowingness 'I am'; later on you embraced the body. Hold on to this only, and don't ask any questions. You came to know yourself, 'I am', to abide in that itself is 'bhakti', the devotion.

Your first step is beingness: embrace the knowledge 'I am' be that.

Your first task is to see the sorrow in you and around you; your next, to long intensely for liberation. The very intensity of longing will guide you; you need no other guide.

Your Guru, your God is the 'I am', with its coming came duality and all activity, stay on the 'I am', you are before the 'I am' appeared.

Your own little body too is full of mysteries and dangers, yet you are not afraid of it, for you take it as your own. What you do not know is that the entire universe is your body, and you need not be afraid of it. You may say you have two bodies: the personal and the universal. The personal comes and goes, the universal is always with you. The entire creation is your universal body. You are so blinded by what is personal, that you do not see the universal. This blindness will not end by itself - it must be undone skilfully and deliberately. When all illusions are understood and abandoned, you reach the error-free and perfect state in which all distinctions between the personal and the universal are no more.

Your own self is your ultimate teacher (sadguru). The outer teacher (guru) is merely a milestone. It is only your inner teacher that will walk with you to the goal, for it is the goal.

For eternal peace you must dwell in yourself, know how this touch of 'I am' has appeared. All other knowledge is of no use in this connection.

In order to not mistakenly hold on to something as 'I am' don't say I am this, I am that; just hold on to yourself, you are, just be.

[My condition is] absolutely steady. Whatever I may do, it stays like a rock - motionless. Once you have awakened into reality, you stay in it. It is self-evident and yet beyond description.

You should identify yourself only with this indwelling knowledge 'I am'. That is all. Sit in meditation by identifying with the 'I am', dwell only on the 'I am'- not merely the words 'I am'.

You should understand this clearly. If one thinks one is the body, one becomes a slave of mind and suffers accordingly. Therefore, you should completely identify yourself with the highest principle in you, which is the knowledge 'I am'. This will elevate you to the status of 'brihaspati' - the guru of gods.

Your being a person is due to the illusion of space and time; you imagine yourself to be at a certain point occupying a certain volume; your personality is due to your self-identification with the body.

Your conviction that you are conscious of a world is the world. The world you perceive is made of consciousness; what you call matter is consciousness itself.

Your fall started with the appearance of that beingness, 'I am'. With the appearance of this knowingness 'I am', the next fall was embracing the body as 'I am'. And then you gathered so many things onto yourself. Hold on to the state of knowing yourself as 'I am' as the truth. All other things you have gathered to yourself are unreal.

[One reaches the Supreme state] by renouncing all lesser desires. As long as you are pleased with the lesser, you cannot have the highest. Whatever pleases you keeps you back. Until you realize the unsatisfactoriness of everything, its transiency and limitation, and collect your energies in one great longing, ever the first step is not made. On the other hand, the integrity of the desire for the Supreme is by itself a call from the Supreme. Nothing, physical or mental, can give you freedom. You are free once you understand that your bondage is of your own making and cease forging the chains that bind you.

'I am' is a quality, an attribute, indicating beingness, but the Self is not a quality. For that Ultimate Self no worldly knowledge is necessary. Words are not called for. But for the sustenance of this beingness, these words and worldly knowledge is necessary.

You need not stop thinking. Just cease being interested. It is disinterestedness that liberates. Don't hold on, that is all.

You observe the heart feeling, the mind thinking, the body acting; the very act of perceiving shows that you are not what you perceive.

You reduce your identification with the body, in that process the knowledge 'I am' which knows itself, will be clear. If you embrace the body sense, there will be a lot of questions. If the knowledge 'you are' is not there, will anybody keep this body? The principle that rejects or gives up the body is your Self.

You see me apparently functioning. In reality, I only look. Whatever is done, is done on the stage. Joy and sorrow, life and death, they all are real to the man in bondage; to me, they are all in the show, as unreal as the show itself. I may perceive the world just like you, but you believe to be in it, while I see it as an iridescent drop in the vast expanse of consciousness.

'I am' is ever fresh. You do need to remember in order to 'be' As a matter of fact, before you can experience anything, there must be the sense of being. At present your being is mixed up with experiencing. All you need to do is to unravel being from the tangle of experiences. Once you have known pure being, without being this or that, you will discern it among experiences, and you will no longer be misled by names and forms.

'I am' is only a few letters. Has anyone been able to keep this 'I am' in his pocket for all time? If whoever feels that 'I am' had knowledge, would he have cared to become this 'I am'? No, he would have said 'I don't want this consciousness'. You are unreal – you know that you are – that is also unreal. This sense of presence is an untruth, it is like a dream.

You must not indulge in forecasts and plans, born of memory and anticipation. It is one of the peculiarities of a gnani that he is not concerned with future. Your concern with future is due to fear of pain and desire for pleasure; to the gnani all is bliss: he is happy with whatever comes.

You must possess that confirmation that you are formless, designless and not only rely on meditation. Always insist on that you are formless, free and not conditioned. You must hammer on this constantly; that is the practice. You must have a strong conviction that conviction means practicing. That conviction means not only 'I am' but it means I am free from the 'I am' also.

You must unlearn everything. God is the end of all desire and knowledge.

You need not get at it, you are it. It will get at you, if you give it a chance. Let go your attachment to the unreal and the real will swiftly and smoothly step into its own. Stop imagining yourself being or doing this or that, and the realization that you are the source and heart of all will dawn upon you.

You need not set it [your mind] right, it will set itself right, as soon as you give up all concern with the past and the future and live entirely in the now.

'I am' is there without saying 'I am'. 'I amness' without thought is love, love is not taken from the 'I amness' The Self becomes manifest when love gets established as the 'I amness'.

'I am' itself is God, the seeking itself is God. In seeking you discover that you are neither the body nor the mind, and the love of the self in you is for the self in all. The two are one. The consciousness in you and the consciousness in me, apparently two, really one, seek unity and that is love. What do you love now? The 'I am'. Give your heart and mind to it, think of nothing else. This when effortless and natural, is the highest state. In it love itself is the lover and the beloved.

You must have a firm conviction that 'I am' is only that 'I am' without body-mind form – the knowledge 'I am' purely. You say all these things, but has the knowledge come within the purview of the knowledge? You must have that full conviction, whatever you may have said, that is the truth and that is 'I am'. There are no techniques, except the technique that 'I am' the firm conviction that 'I am' means 'I am' only, abidance in 'I'. Don't practice this thing, only develop your conviction.

You must know what this 'I am' principle is. It appears spontaneously and with its appearance begins the riddle of conceptual life.

You must maintain this knowledge 'I am' in proper order. All the dirt, which is not the towel, should be removed. Similarly 'I am' is the tool through which you get all the knowledge. You worship that 'I am', remove all the adulteration, the dirt.

You must meditate on that 'I am' without holding on to the body and mind. As you nursed at your mother's breast when you were a baby, so must you nurse at this 'I am', the knowledge of your beingness. Remember and meditate on this also 'I have no fear, I am beyond fear'. I am telling you that this fear will gradually lessen and will go completely, because I say so. The medicine for that fear is my word.

You must meditate on the 'I am' without holding on to the body-mind, the 'I am' is the first ignorance, persist on it and you will go beyond it.

'I am' itself is the world; it contains the entire world, that should be your conviction. Just as in a dream, when you feel that you are awake, but actually you are not and your world at that time is the dream world. Similarly this knowingness (in the waking state) contains this so-called real world; that conviction must come. The truth is that there is no difference between (dream) consciousness and (waking) consciousness, although they appear to be greatly different; all consciousness is one.

The beginning of concepts started with the primary concept 'I am'. Having wandered through all the concepts, and rejected them, you have to get rid of this last or the first concept.

The very core of all atoms is permeated by that knowledge 'I am'. Embrace all the atoms of the universe with the feeling that all of them have come inside us in the form of the knowledge 'I am'.

You must analyze 'death', the meaning of this common parlance. At the time that death occurs, the vital breath quits the body, gradually leaves the body. At the same time as the vital breath, the mind and the language also go out. Simultaneously, this quality of 'I am', this 'sattva-guna', the quality of beingness, also departs or goes into oblivion. Only I, the Absolute remains. Stay put there only; nothing happens to I, the Absolute.

You must become initiated into the understanding of what I am expounding to you. I am telling about the seed of 'Brahman'. You have to understand that I am planting the 'Brahma' seed in you. That 'Brahma' seed is your 'I amness' (Beingness), which sprouts into manifestation. That 'Brahman' ('I am') state does not require anything to eat, it has no hunger, because 'Brahman' alone embraces everything and all manifestation is 'Brahman'. I am trying to raise you to that state. Do not think that you can become a realized soul only by listening to a few talks. You have to forget everything and merge with 'Brahman'.

You must come to a firm decision. You must forget the thought that you are the body and be only the knowledge 'I am', which has no form, no name. Just be. When you stabilize in that beingness it will give all the knowledge and all the secrets to you, and when the secrets are given to you, you transcend the beingness, and you, the Absolute will know that you are also not the consciousness. Having gained all this knowledge, having understood what is what, a kind of quietude prevails, a tranquility. Beingness is transcended, but beingness is available.

You must find your own way. Unless you find it yourself, it will not be your own way and will take you nowhere. Earnestly live your truth as you have found it, act on the little you have understood. It is earnestness that will take you through, not cleverness - your own or another's.

You must give up the identity with the body. Abidance in that knowledge 'I am' which does not identify with the body-mind is the spiritual light. Self-love and 'I am' without words are the same. The sickness may come and go, but the self-love does not go.

'I amness' and Maya are the watcher and the Lila respectively. The 'I am' is not involved in any of the activity. I am expounding this knowledge from the 'I am' level, though my normal state observes the 'I amness'.

'I amness' is there provided these stages (waking or sleep) are there, by itself it cannot be. Simultaneously, all these three stages are a product of food essence. In the absence of body sense, is there any community of waking and sleep states? Have this affirmation, forget spirituality and dwell there (in the 'I am').

You have to transcend the 'I am' to enter the concept-free Parabrahman state, where you do not even know you are!

You know only what is in your consciousness. What you claim exists outside conscious experience is inferred.

You know you are sitting here. Be attentive to that knowledge only. Just be in your beingness. That knowingness 'I am' has created the entire universe. Hold on to that; nothing has to be done. Once you recognize that principle it becomes tranquil. Become one with that and all your needs will be satisfied.

You know you are sitting here; you know you are, do you require any special effort to hold on to that 'you are'? You know you are; abide only in that. The 'I am' principle without words, that itself is the God of all 'Ishwaras'.

You know you are. Because you know you are, everything is happening. Go to that knowledge 'I am'. When you understand what that 'I amness' is, then the shell of mystery is broken.

'I amness' is without ego. The subsequent products are the mind and the ego. The quality of 'I amness' or Beingness is intuition and inspiration. Just like when you have seed and plant it, it must sprout. Similarly the quality of Beingness must sprout.

Along with that the whole manifestation, the entire Universe, has come upon it. Otherwise, there is absolutely nothing. And out of many 'jnanis', there will only be a rare one who knows the real nature of this primary concept.

'Jnana-yoga' means to inquire how this 'I amness' and the world came about. To realize that 'I amness' and the world are the same is 'jnana-yoga'. Here the knowledge 'I am' should subside in itself.

You can do what you like, as long as you do not take yourself to be the body and the mind. It is not so much a question of actual giving up the body and all that goes with it, as a clear understanding that you are not the body, a sense of aloofness, of emotional non-involvement.

You can observe the observation, but not the observer. You know you are the ultimate observer by direct insight, not by a logical process based on observation. You are what you are, but you know what you are not. The self is known as being, the not-self is known as transient. But in reality all is in the mind. The observed, observation and observer are mental constructs. The self alone is.

You did not have the concept 'I am' in the course of the nine months in the womb. Understanding this state of affairs, the concept 'I am' comes spontaneously and goes spontaneously. Amazingly, when it appears, it is accepted as real. All subsequent misconceptions arise from the feeling of reality in the 'I amness'. Try to stabilize in the primary concept 'I am', in order to lose that and with it all other concepts. Why am I totally free? Because I have understood the unreality of that 'I am'.

You have 'to be' before anything else can be, your sense of 'presence' or the feeling 'I am' is really fundamental to anything that has to follow.

You have to be one with the Self, the 'I am'. If you say knowledge, it is just the same as information. If necessary discard the words 'I am'. Even without words you know that 'you are'. Do not say or even think that 'you are', just be aware of the presence without thinking about it.

If this is indeed your conviction then you are the 'Parabrahman'. This thing aside, you should discover how this news 'I am' – the knowledge of your existence – appeared and at what moment. Go to the source of it and find out.

You are the Self, here and now. Leave the mind alone, stand aware and unconcerned, and you will realize that to stand alert and detached, watching events come and go, is an aspect of your real nature.

You are worrying because of the intellect, but you have only to continue in that 'I am' with faith, you have nothing else to do. You are likely to miss that incident if you try to use your intellect. Just let it happen. Hold on to the feeling 'I am'; don't pollute that state by holding on to the body sense.

You base yourself on the body that you are now, and don't understand its root. That is why we think we are this body, and for that you must do meditation. What is meditation? Meditation is not this body-mind meditating as an individual, but it is this knowledge 'I am', this consciousness, meditating on itself. Then the consciousness will unfold its own meaning.

You came here and I talk to you but I am not concerned whether you come or go. I am totally independent. I, as the Absolute, do not need the consciousness. Total independence is merely to apprehend and understand. My apparent dependence is on this consciousness which says 'I am'. It is this sentience which enables me to perceive you. This concept I did not have but even then I existed. I was there before this consciousness appeared.

You can become a night watchman and live happily. It is what you are inwardly that matters. Your inner peace and joy you have to earn. It is much more difficult than earning money. No university can teach you to be yourself.

'Satva' is only the essence of the five elements and in that is the knowledge 'I am'. All that is still of the five elements, so how did this come about? Then my Guru told me, 'this is what you are', the whole story; so from my own experience I know that it is all ignorance.

'Upadro'(meaning disturbance in Marathi), is the source of trouble. In this 'upadro', in this primary essence, lies the knowledge 'I am' – you know that you are. This quality of beingness ('sattvaguna'), the knowledge 'I am' cannot tolerate itself. It cannot stand itself, alone, just knowing itself. Therefore that 'rajoguna' is there… it takes the beingness for a ride in various activities, so that it does not dwell on itself; it is very difficult to sustain that state. And 'tamoguna' is the basest quality, it claims authorship or doership for all those activities conducted through 'rajoguna'. This is the play happening in these three gunas (qualities). Again understand, you are experiencing this 'sattvaguna', the knowledge 'I am. This 'I amness' is experienced by you, the Absolute, but you are not the 'I amness'.

You are sitting here: 'you are', prior to words. Now the hearsay goes 'I am', 'I am' means the flow of the mind has started. Now whatever you say with that 'I amness', through the mind about 'you', you have represented as yourself. But that is not so.

You are so used to support of concepts that when your concepts leave you, although it is your true state, you get frightened and try to cling to them again. This is the meeting point of that immanent principle and the Eternal, the borderland. Why is the intellect puzzled here? That beingness which you are experiencing is melting away. When the concept of 'I am' goes, intellect also goes. So the intellect gets that frightening experience of 'I am going'.

You are the knowledge ('I am') and you don't have any shape or form whatsoever. You are impersonal. You are comprehensive. You are the manifest, the Universal Consciousness. What would happen if you went in search of that Consciousness? The seeker would disappear in the search, because the 'I amness' is all there is.

You are the knowledge 'I am'. So if you want to worship, worship that knowledge 'I am'. Be devoted to that 'I amness' only. When you do that, other rituals become redundant and useless. Finally when you realize that everything is useless, everything is 'Brahman', it means you are at the 'Parabrahman' level, the absolute level. When at that level, you will envision everything as useless, including the 'Brahman' because the 'Brahman' is also reduced to illusion. Therefore all these talks, including my own will be reduced to illusion when you reach the highest.

You are the Reality beyond the 'I am', you are the 'Parabrahma'. Meditate on this and remember this, finally this idea, too, shall leave you. Understand the 'I am', transcend it and realize the Absolute.

'You are', that is 'Ishwara, that is you. I am giving you instructions regarding your 'beginningless being' but you prefer to be that monkey form. You are not prepared to leave that form.

'You' are above the waking and dreaming states, because those are only expressions of your Beingness. The waking and dreaming states pertain only to your 'I amness'. We are only able to observe because of the 'I amness'. When the 'I amness' is not there the tool to observe is also not there. If you are deep inside everything is gone! And there is no 'I am'. Then the 'I am' merges in the Absolute.

You are neither the body nor in the body. There is no such thing as body. You have grievously misunderstood yourself. To understand rightly, investigate.

You are not the personality or the individual. The quintessence of this food, which in turn is the outcome of the five-elemental play, is the taste 'I am'. 'I am' is not a personality or an individual. I am addressing that principle, that touch of 'I am', that consciousness which is the product of the food essence body.

You are quite knowledgeable; now understand this; if you think you are dying, it shows that you still identify with your body and that your knowledge 'I am' has not merged in itself, which also indicates that you have not attained 'jnana-yoga'. Your spiritual knowledge therefore smacks of impurity. While you are actually the manifest knowledge 'I am', you cling to a body as yourself; this is the impurity.

You are really in search of yourself, without knowing it. You are love-longing for the love-worthy, the perfect lovable. Due to ignorance you are looking for it in the world of opposites and contradictions. When you find it within, your search will be over.

You are separate from 'I am'. 'I am' is itself an illusion. The knowledge 'I am' and the world are tricks of Maya. There is no substance in them. There are no words actually; you speak words for your satisfaction.

A 'jnani' knows that he has realized when he recognizes his knowingness, which is the sense of 'I am'. Right here and now you are in the realized state. But you try to judge it through desires and mind-concepts, hence your inability to apperceive it and abide in it. In the 'jnani' state, there is no need for anything, not even to know oneself. You are attached to the body-senses; therefore even though you may attain an age of hundred years, you still would crave for more years.

A body maybe dark, fair, tall or short, but the indwelling principle – which is the knowledge 'I am' has no color or dimension, just like the vital breath and mind. It is merely a 'sense of presence' a feeling of effulgence. And mind functions like its vehicle or medium for executing worldly activities.

A man who is given a stone and assured that it is a priceless diamond will be mightily pleased until he realizes his mistake; in the same way, pleasures lose their tang and pains their barb when the self is known. Both are seen as they are - conditional responses, mere reactions.

You are afraid because you have assumed something as 'I am', which actually you are not. Suppose you find a diamond ring on the road and you pocket it. Since it is not yours, a fear overcomes you. When you put on an identity that is not yours, you are afraid, but when you are the pure 'I amness' only, there is no fear. Presently you are this 'I am', but this 'I am' is not the truth. Whatever you are prior to the appearance of the 'I am', that is your real nature.

You are always the Supreme. But your attention is fixed on things, physical or mental. When your attention is off a thing and not yet fixed on another, in the interval you are pure being. When through the practice of discrimination and detachment (viveka-vairagya), you lose sight of sensory and mental states, pure being emerges as the natural state. By focusing the mind on "I am", on the sense of being, "I am so-and-so" dissolves; "am a witness only" remains and that too submerges in "I am all". Then the all becomes the One, and the One yourself.

You are dependent for your living on the strength of your body that it gets from the food you eat and the essence of this food and food body is this consciousness 'I am'. Your beingness is within you not somewhere else.

You are like a child with a lollypop in its mouth. You may feel happy for a moment by being totally self-centered, but it is enough to have a good look at human faces to perceive the universality of suffering. Even your own happiness is so vulnerable and short-lived, at the mercy of a bank-crash, or a stomach ulcer. It is just a moment of respite, a mere gap between two sorrows. Real happiness is not vulnerable, because it does not depend on circumstances.

You are neither the 'I am' nor its activities, you as the Absolute are none of these. Be a true devotee, by abiding in the knowledge 'I am' thereby transcending the experience of death to attain immortality.

A quiet mind is all you need. All else will happen rightly, once your mind is quiet. As the sun on rising makes the world active, so does self-awareness affect changes in the mind. In the light of calm and steady self-awareness, inner energies wake up and work miracles without any effort on your part.

After all, what do you really want? Not perfection; you are already perfect. What you seek is to express in action what you are. For this you have a body and a mind. Take them in hand and make them serve you.

After deep sleep, as soon as consciousness dawns on you of 'I am' – that is the witness. Before that moment you did not know that you are, there was no witness, no knowledge of 'I am'.

All change affects the mind only. To be what you are, you must go beyond the mind, into your own being. It is immaterial what is the mind that you leave behind, provided you leave it behind for good. This again is not possible without self-realization. Self-realization definitely comes first. The mind cannot go beyond itself by itself. It must explode. The explosive power comes from the real. But you are well advised to have your mind ready for it.

Worship the beingness, which is nothing but suffering. Worship misery and it will become less and less. It will also help you to get rid of misery; this 'I am' is itself misery, make any use of it as you like. If you like you may take it as Prarabdha (Destiny).

Worship the knowledge 'I am' as God, as your Guru. The knowledge 'I am' is your Guru. Be in it. Do you see the image of yourself in the mirror first, or do you know you are prior to that? Which is first? If you are not, can you see your image in the mirror? Give up trying to evaluate the real I or the counterfeit I, but associate with the 'Brahman', I am the 'Brahman'.

You abide in that knowledge 'I am'. You should understand that your destination is your own self, the 'I am'. It is the very source of everything; That 'I am' is to be realized. Because 'you are', the consciousness is. Before you say 'I am' you already are. 'I am' – the word or the 'I am' feeling that you get inside you – is not eternal. But you are eternal and ancient.

You are 'That' only, prior to them (concepts and memory) is the 'I am', further still when you recede, is the Absolute. But most people die with memory and concepts. Who understands that memory is not operating today? It's the knowledge 'I am'. Surrender to the beingness, from it all movement happens; go to the source of the movement which is the beingness. Hammer it into yourself that your own beingness is the parent of the entire manifestation. Beingness will help you in abiding in itself, beingness is observed by the Ultimate (the Absolute) that has no senses, no eyes, but witnessing just happens. I am introducing you to your own beingness, the first stage is to meditate on the beingness, abide in it.

You are a man because you identify with the body. If you do not identify with the body, what sex are you? After leaving the body, the vital breath and the 'I am' merge into the substratum. Then where is man or woman?

All desires must be given up, because by desiring you take the shape of your desires. When no desires remain, you revert to your natural state.

All directions are within the mind. I am not asking you to look in any particular direction. Just look away from all that happens in your mind and bring it to the feeling 'I am'. The 'I am' is not a direction. It is the negation of all directions. Ultimately even the 'I am' will have to go for you need not keep asserting what is obvious. Bringing the mind to the feeling 'I am' merely helps turning the mind away from everything else.

Without the intake of food, there is no opportunity to say 'I am', out of the essence of the earth sprouts vegetation and out of that sprouts the 'I am', realize this without eyesight or intellect. That principle likes to cry, enjoy, and laugh, but you are not that, realize this only. Become one with the 'I am', then you can transcend it, then 'I the Absolute' am not the 'I am'.

All experience is necessarily transient. But the ground of all experience is immovable. Nothing that may be called an event will last. But some events purify the mind and some stain it. Moments of deep insight and all-embracing love purify the mind, while desires and fears, envies and anger, blind beliefs and intellectual arrogance pollute and dull the psyche.

All hangs on the idea 'I am'. Examine it very thoroughly. It lies at the root of every trouble. This 'I am' idea was not born with you. You could have lived very well without it. It came later due to your self-identification with the body. It created an illusion of separation where there was none. It made you a stranger in your own world alien and inimical. Without the sense of 'I am' life goes on. There are moments when we are without the sense of 'I am', at peace and happy. With the return of 'I am', trouble starts.

Without this 'I amness' the Absolute does not know that 'It is'. Watching is not deliberate. Watching happens to the Absolute only with the appearance of 'I amness'. The 'I amness', like binoculars, must be there and available for watching to happen.

Witnessing happens to the state prior to your saying the words 'I am'.

All I can say is 'I am', all else is inference. But the inference has become a habit. Destroy all habits of thinking and sleeping. The sense 'I am' is a manifestation of a deeper cause, which you may call self, God, Reality or by any other name. The 'I am' is in the world but it is the key which can open the door out of the world.

Witnessing is natural and no problem. The problem is excessive interest, leading to self-identification. Whatever you are engrossed in, you take to be real.

Words betray their hollowness. The real cannot be described, it must be experienced. I cannot find better words for what I know. What I say may sound ridiculous. But what the words try to convey is the highest truth. All is one, however much we quibble. And all is done to please the one source and goal of every desire, whom we all know as the 'I am'.

All is secondary to the tiny little thing which is the 'I am'. Without the 'I am' there is nothing. All knowledge is about the 'I am'. False ideas about this 'I am' lead to bondage, right knowledge leads to freedom and happiness. The 'I am' denotes the inner while 'there is' denotes the outer; both are based on the sense of being.

All multiplicity is manifested from the Ishwara principle; it is sprouting from the 'I am' principle, Ishwara, or 'I am' is the manifest principle. If you don't forget yourself for four days, you will die. You did not know you were, suddenly you felt 'you are' and with 'I amness' you started counting age. When exactly you felt that 'you are'? Dwell there, ponder over it.

With the arrival of the consciousness, it occurs to you that you are; simultaneously, 'I am' occurs to you or in your attention. So when the consciousness is not there, attention is also not there. Subsequent to the arrival of consciousness and attention, everything else crept in. The Absolute state is prior to consciousness; it means the unborn state. Since the 'Parabrahman' is the unborn state, prior to consciousness, can it have an iota of knowledge?

All talk of 'gnana' is a sign of ignorance. It is the mind that imagines that it does not know and then comes to know. Reality knows nothing of these contortions. Even the idea of God as the Creator is false. Do I owe my being to another being? Because 'I am' all 'is'.

All that happens, happens in and to the mind, not to the source of the 'I am'. Once you realize that all happens by itself (call it destiny or the will of God or mere accident), you remain as witness only, understanding and enjoying, but not perturbed.

With the arrival of the primary concept 'I am', time began, with its departure time will end; you the Absolute are not the primary concept 'I am'.

With the transcendence of the knowledge 'I am', the Absolute prevails. The state is called 'Parabrahman', while the knowledge 'I am' is termed Brahman. This knowledge 'I am' or the beingness is illusion only. Therefore, when Brahman is transcended, only the 'Parabrahman' is, in which there is not even a trace of the knowledge 'I am'.

All the glories will come with mere dwelling on the feeling 'I am'. It is the simple that is certain, not the complicated. Somehow, people do not trust the simple, the easy, the always available. Why not give an honest trial to what I say? It may look very small and insignificant, but it is like a seed that grows into a mighty tree.

With what identity do you judge me or judge yourself? You entertain the idea that you are going to have different births, I don't believe in any such stories. I know 'I' never was, that 'I amness' was never there for me. I am the unborn state.

With whatever concepts you hold on you go to a Guru, if he is a Jnani he gets rid of all your concepts. But what is the main concept on which all depends? It's the 'I am', the 'I am' is itself a concept. It is a basic source from which all other concepts flow. Getting a firm conviction about yourself is to become a Sadguru (the one beyond the 'I am').Whatever is termed as Parabrahman – the Absolute – is your true Self.

All these things in the objective world are inseparable from their attributes. An attribute by its very nature depends upon attributes. That knowledge 'I am', is also an attribute, therefore, the 'I amness' one way or another, also has to depend on something.

All thinking is in duality. In identity, no thought survives.

Who says that he is alive? Find out, who is the Witness who 'knows' that he is alive? This is awareness of one's existence, 'I am' prior to thought. Who says 'I am alive', who says 'I am not alive', what is that? 'I am' is not something that can be put into words; it is the knowledge, the Awareness before thought. You have to just 'Be'.

Why not investigate the very idea of body? Does the mind appear in the body or the body in the mind? Surely there must be a mind to conceive the "I-am-the-body" idea. A body without a mind cannot be 'my body'. 'My body' is invariably absent when the mind is in abeyance. It is also absent when the mind is deeply engaged in thoughts and feelings.

Why not turn away from the experience to the experiencer and realize the full import of the only true statement you can make: 'I am'. Just keep in mind the feeling 'I am', merge in it, till your mind and feeling become one. By repeated attempts you will stumble on the right balance of attention and affection and your mind will be firmly established in the thought-feeling 'I am'. Whatever you think, say or do, this sense of immutable and affectionate being remains as the ever-present background of the mind.

With firm conviction, you abide in this knowledge 'I am' only; bereft of body-mind sense, only 'I am'. If you dwell therein, if you be that only, in due course it will get mature. And it will reveal to you all the knowledge. And you need not go to anybody else.

With greatest interest you get absorbed in your Self. By giving attention only to your 'I' consciousness you can reach it. Without giving attention to the body but to the sense 'I am'.

All this conceptual cycle is created by you because you have the concept 'I am', which you must eradicate yourself. When you are in deep sleep is there any experience of pleasure and pain or birth and death? What does that mean? It means that the concept 'I am' has vanished.

Who has the knowledge 'I am'? Somebody in you knows the knowledge 'I am', who is it? It is very obvious that you know you are, but what or who is it that knows you are?

All this is the play of concepts. The primary concept 'I am' appears spontaneously. It likes 'I am'; it loves that 'I am' state. Devouring ever more concepts, it gets totally enmeshed in them. And what is the source of all concepts? This primary feeling 'I am'. But never forget the fact that it itself is a concept, time-bound. And so it is all mental entertainment.

All this knowledge has dawned on me, I am not the knowledge.

Who is a Jnani? A Jnani is one who has come to a conclusion about the raw material of the 'I am' and that he stands apart from it. You presume that you have a lot of knowledge, yet you have not been able to get rid of your identity, but even if you keep in mind just two words ('I am'), your job is done.

Who is going to give you eternal peace? It is only the sun, the 'I am'. If you embrace that Self-effulgent sun everything else will go, but you will prevail eternally.

All this process of communication, expounding, etc., will go on so long as this conscious presence is available, and all this is to merely satisfy the concept 'I am', and you the Absolute, are not the primary concept 'I am'.

Who is it that needs to understand this the most, the knowledge that 'I am'? If you listen carefully and imbibe the principles, you will get rid of this body-mind sense and dwell only in the 'I amness' (Beingness). In order to know the link between 'I am' and 'I am not', hold on only to the 'I amness' without words, 'just be'. When hailed, you respond, there is somebody within you that becomes aware of the call and the need to respond. That being is the 'I am' and he has been there even before that awareness appeared.

Who is talking? Who is walking? Who is sitting? These are the expressions of the chemical 'I am'. Are you that chemical? You talk about heaven and hell, this Mahatma or that one, but how about you? Who are you? You are not this chemical 'I am'.

All those praises sung by the 'Vedas' are only for that tiny little pinch 'I am'. The moment you start making a design of that 'I amness' you are getting into deep waters. This incense holder is silver; you have the knowledge that it is silver. What is the shape, color, or design of that knowledge? If all knowledge is formless, could there be a form, design or color to the knowledge 'I am'? Could it be subject to sin or merit?

When you were unaware of this message of 'I am' how did you function? The question I put, nobody can answer. All of your great scholars, people with a lot of knowledge, have gone into quietude.

Whenever a thought or emotion of desire or fear comes to your mind, just turn away from it. I'm not talking of suppression. Just refuse attention.

All this profound talk is nothing but mental entertainment. As you go further into spirituality you will realize that 'I am' is the very God or soul of an infinite number of universes, but the 'I am' is again entertainment. All my talks are conceptual entertainment.

Whenever there is a problem you ask: 'let us find the state of affairs as they are', don't try to bluff, and then the solution comes. So in this fraudulent play of the manifest world I went on to find the actual position, the 'I amness' means world manifestation and it is a time bound state, so why should I bother? Presently 'I amness' is bubbling and challenging, but all this is time bound, pride will go along with the 'I am' (So Hum), later on, 'no-I am' (No Hum).

Where is the need of changing anything? The mind is changing anyhow all the time. Look at your mind dispassionately; this is enough to calm it. When it is quiet, you can go beyond it. Do not keep it busy all the time. Stop it, and just be. If you give it rest, it will settle down and recover its purity and strength. Constant thinking makes it decay.

Where there is the vital breath, the knowledge 'I am' is present.

All waiting is futile. To depend on time to solve our problems is self-delusion. The future, left to itself merely repeats the past. Change can only happen now, never in the future.

All your experiences and visions depend on your knowledge 'I am' and this itself is going to dissolve. For this knowledge there are no customers, no devotees, because they want something concrete in their hand, but when your knowingness itself is going to dissolve, is it possible to hold on to something?

All your moments of spirituality are based on the 'I am the body' idea. This knowledge 'I am' is going to remain for a short period. This will be very clear to you when you remain in your real position. Until then accept whatever concepts of spirituality you like. Until you know your true state you will accept all the hearsays because you don't know the truth.

Along with the knowledge 'I am' appears space and the world. When the knowledge 'I am' departs the world is liquidated.

When you remain in the 'I am' you will realize everything else is useless, and then you are Parabrahman, the Absolute.

When you say you sit for meditation, the first thing to be done is to understand that it is not this body identification that is sitting for meditation, but this knowledge 'I am', this consciousness, which is sitting in meditation and is meditating on itself. When this is finally understood, then it becomes easy. When this consciousness, this conscious presence, merges in itself, the state of 'samadhi' ensues. It is the conceptual feeling that I exist that disappears and merges into the beingness itself. So this conscious presence also gets merged into that knowledge, that beingness – that is 'samadhi'.

When you see the world you see God. There is no seeing God apart from the world. Beyond the world to see God is to be God. The light by which you see the world, which is God is the tiny little spark: 'I am', apparently so small and yet the first and the last in every act of knowing and loving.

When you sit in deep meditation, your sense of being is totally infused with the knowledge 'I am' only. In such a state it will be revealed to you intuitively as to how and why your sense of 'I amness' emerged. Consciousness, beingness, sense of being, 'I amness', all are the same in you, prior to emanation of any words.

Any embodied person with the knowledge 'I am' carries on his activities in the world with the name only. That inner core, the 'I am' has no shackles. Once it is understood that I am that 'I am' only, and not this shackled form, then no liberation is called for, that itself is liberation.

When you sit quiet and watch yourself, all kinds of things may come to the surface. Do nothing about them, don't react to them; as they have come so will they go, by themselves. All that matters is mindfulness, total awareness of oneself, or rather of one's mind.

Appearance and disappearance, birth and death these are qualities of 'I am', they do not belong to you, the Absolute.

Apply your mind, go back in time and try to recollect the moment when for the first time it dawned on you that 'you are' or 'I am'. This nascent 'I am' is without words or non-verbal.

When you feel that you are separate from the feeling 'I am' isn't there something or someone who knows that there is a difference?

Are we all here because of our volition to be born or has this knowingness appeared in us unknowingly? This beingness has come to you without your knowledge, but you are using it according to your own volition. I want to sentence that individuality to death. Is it not justice that I pronounce this sentence? So think carefully. The individuality must go. 'Parabrahman' is purest justice and Truth.

Are you not even before you have spoken the words 'I am'? Stay put there only. There begins your spirituality, the foremost 'you', 'I am' without words, before the beginning of words. Be there; out of that grows the experience 'I am'. Witnessing happens to that principle which prior to your saying the words 'I am'. There is no such thing as deliberate witnessing. Witnessing just happens, by itself.

When you follow my advice and try to keep the mind on the notion of 'I am' only, you become fully aware of your mind and its vagaries. Awareness being lucid harmony ('sattwa') in action dissolves dullness and quietens the restlessness of the mind and gently but steadily changes its very substance. This change need not be spectacular; it maybe hardly noticeable; and yet it is a deep and fundamental shift from darkness to light from inadvertence to awareness.

When you get established in the Beingness there no thoughts or words. You are everything and everything is You. Later even that ceases to exist. Krishna made Arjuna realize that the whole world is Krishna. He realized that the knowledge 'I am', which means the manifestation of the entire universe, spontaneously appeared on him.

When you got yourself separated from the Absolute with this identity 'I am', you felt fragmented, isolated, and that is why your demands started. In the Absolute there are no needs, only the Absolute prevails. The truth is total Brahman only, nothing else but Brahman. In a total Brahman state arose the touch of beingness, 'I am', and with that, separation started, otherness has come. But this 'I amness' is not just a small principle, that itself is the 'moolmaya', the primary illusion.

When you meditate on the knowledge 'I am', which is the beginning of knowledge, how can there be any questions? It is not with the body identification that you should sit for meditation. It is the knowledge 'I am' that is meditating on itself.

As long as one is conscious, there will be pain and pleasure. You cannot fight pain and pleasure on the level of consciousness. To go beyond them, you must go beyond consciousness, which is possible only when you look at consciousness as something that happens to you, and not in you, as something external, alien, superimposed. Then, suddenly you are free of consciousness, really alone, with nothing to intrude. And that is your true state. Consciousness is an itching rash that makes you scratch. Of course, you cannot step out of consciousness, for the very stepping out is in consciousness. But if you learn to look at your consciousness as a sort of fever, personal and private, in which you are enclosed like a chick in its shell, out of this very attitude will come the crisis which will break the shell.

As long as we imagine ourselves to be separate personalities, one quite apart from another, we cannot grasp reality, which is essentially impersonal. First we must know ourselves as witnesses only, dimensionless and timeless centers of observation, and then realize that immense ocean of pure awareness, which is both mind and matter and beyond both.

When you are the space you are no more the body, but whatever is contained in that space you are. You are now manifest – whatever is known – the space. This space is known as 'chidakash'. In 'chidakash this knowingness is 'I am'. In the highest 'Paramakash' there is no is or is not, It transcends everything.

As long as you are engrossed in the world, you are unable to know yourself: to know yourself, turn away your attention from the world and turn it within.

As long as you are interested in your present way of living, you will not abandon it. Discovery cannot come as long as you cling to the familiar. It is only when you realize fully the immense sorrow of your life and revolt against it that a way out can be found.

When you become one with that knowledge you will realize that the knowledge 'I am' is the very Guru of the universe. Don't make use of anything except the knowledge 'I am'. Forget everything else. Consider a magnificent tree with many branches and leaves. Go to the root and not the branches.

When you began knowing that you are, you did a lot of mischief, but when the 'I am' is not there, there is no question of mischief.

As long as you are wearing this concept 'I am' you will be involved with all the concepts. When this concept 'I am' departs there will be no memory left that 'I was' and 'I had' those experiences; the very memory will be erased.

When you demand nothing of the world, nor of God, when you want nothing, seek nothing, expect nothing, then the Supreme State will come to you uninvited and unexpected.

When you desire and fear, and identify yourself with your feelings, you create sorrow and bondage. When you create, with love and wisdom, and remain unattached to your creations, the result is harmony and peace. But whatever be the condition of your mind, in what way does it reflect on you? It is only your self-identification with your mind that makes you happy or unhappy. Rebel against your slavery to your mind, see your bonds as self-created and break the chains of attachment and revulsion. Keep in mind your goal of freedom, until it dawns on you that you are already free, that freedom is not something in the distant future to be earned with painful efforts, but perennially one's own, to be used! Liberation is not an acquisition but a matter of courage, the courage to believe that you are free already and to act on it.

As long as you have all sorts of ideas about yourself, you know yourself through the mist of these ideas; to know yourself as you are, give up all ideas. You cannot imagine the taste of pure water, you can only discover it by abandoning all flavorings.

As long as you identify with the body-mind you are conditioned. Once you stabilize in the knowledge 'I am' unconditionally you are the manifest 'I amness' – no more an individual. In the manifested state of 'I amness' there is no question of your doing, because you are no more an individual. Whatever happens, happens in your consciousness. Whatever happens through this, you also know it will happen, but there is no question of doing or being anything.

When this beingness goes, the Absolute will not know 'I am'. Appearance and disappearance, birth and death, these are qualities of beingness; they are not your qualities.

When this concept 'I am' departs there will be no memory left that 'I was' and 'I had' those experiences, the very memory will be erased.

When the truth came out, it was found that in a certain atom the entire Universe is contained. And what is that atom? It is the beingness, the knowledge 'I am'. That contains the whole Universe.

When you are convinced that 'all of Consciousness is my Self', when the conviction is firmly embedded, then only will the question of the next elevation arise.

When you are in deep sleep and you feel that you are awake, the dream world appears simultaneously. With the 'I am', the world appears in the waking and dream states.

As long as you take yourself to be a person, a body and a mind, separate from the stream of life, having a will of its own, pursuing its own aims, you are living merely on the surface, and whatever you do will be short-lived and of little value, mere straw to feed the flames of vanity.

As self-identification with the body-mind is the poison that brings bondage, seek liberation by seeing that oneself is not anything personal or perceivable.

When the 'I am' goes all that remains is the Absolute, give all your attention to the 'I am'.

When the 'I amness' appears spontaneously, like a bolt of lightning, the illusion of Self-love is broken into five basic elements, space, air, earth, fire and water. But this Self-love, the 'I am' manifests itself as Sattva Guna to the one who accepts this as a natural process. When it is used for achieving something in the world it is referred to as Rajas Guna. When it is used to take credit for achievements, it is referred to as Tamas Guna.

When the body dies, the kind of life you live now, succession of physical and mental events, comes to an end. It can end even now, without waiting for the death of the body. It is enough to shift attention to the Self and keep it there. All happens as if there is a mysterious power that creates and moves everything. Realize that you are not the mover, only the observer, and you will be at peace. Of course not [that power is not separate from you]. But you must begin by being the dispassionate observer. Then only will you realize your full being as the universal lover and actor. As long as you are enmeshed in the tribulations of a particular personality, you can see nothing beyond it.

When the body is born, all kinds of things happen to it, and you take part in them because you take yourself to be the body. You are like the man in the cinema house, laughing and crying with the picture, though knowing fully well that he is all the time in his seat and the picture is but the play of light. It is enough to shift attention from the screen to oneself to break the spell.

When the meditator forgets himself totally in meditation, it is 'vishranti' which means complete relaxation ending in total forgetfulness. This is the blissful state, where there is no need for words, concepts or even the sense of 'I am'. The state does not know 'it is' and is beyond happiness and suffering and altogether beyond words; it is called the 'Parabrahman' – a non-experiential state.

As you cannot see your face, but only its reflection in the mirror, so you can know only your image reflected in the stainless mirror of pure awareness. See the stains and remove them. The nature of the perfect mirror is such that you cannot see it. Whatever you can see is bound to be a stain. Turn away from it, give it up, know it as unwanted. All perceivables are stains.

At first 'no one' is. Instantly, one is, and then two. The subject of the talk is: How did these two reduce to one, and finally to nothing? Out of nothingness spontaneously the sense of beingness is felt - this is one. Later, when the sense of beingness knows 'I am' duality begins. Then after the duality has arisen, the sense of being identifies with the form, and so on. Actually to refer to the sense of being as 'one', is not quite correct. Since in this state only the sense of being prevails, where is the need to say even 'one'? With the appearance of otherness (duality), both no.1 and no.2 appear simultaneously. To say 'something is', 'I' must be there first. If 'I' am not, I cannot say 'something is'. So the fundamental principle of spirituality is that 'I must be there, before anything else can be.

At most I would say 'you worship that 'I am' principle, be one with it and that would disclose all the knowledge'. That's all I will say, but the subtlest part is this, from deep sleep to waking state. To abide in that you must have an intensely peaceful state. In that state witnessing of the waking state happens. You must go to that limit, but it is very difficult.

At present you identify yourself with your body and mind. Therefore, in the initial stages of your spiritual practice, you should reject the identity by imbibing the principle that 'I am' is the vital breath and the consciousness only and not the body and mind. In the later stages, the vital breath and the consciousness – that is the knowledge 'I am' – merge in one's ultimate nature.

When I pleased my 'I amness' by understanding it, only then did I come to know this 'I amness' and in the process also discovered that 'I' the Absolute, am not that 'I am'. Stay put at one place.

At present you wrongly identify yourself as the body. Body is given a certain name; that is 'you'; you consider it to be like that. But I say that in this body, consciousness is present, or the knowledge 'I am' as I call it, is there. You should identify yourself as this knowledge. That is all.

When I repeat: 'I am', 'I am', I merely assert and re-assert an everpresent fact. You get tired of my words because you do not see the living truth behind them. Contact it and you will find the full meaning of words and of silence, both.

When I say 'I am', I do not mean a separate entity with a body as its nucleus; I mean the totality of being, the ocean of consciousness, the entire universe of all that is known. I have nothing to desire for I am complete forever.

When I talk I refer to the 'I am' knowledge and not to me personally. As long as you are attached to and identified with the body you will never have peace. But once you get rid of the body attachment you could be the king and ruler of the world, yet still be at peace.

At present, 'I am' is in the beingness state. But, when I do not have the knowingness of the 'I am' illusion, then the 'Poornabrahman' or 'Parabrahman' state prevails. In the absence of the touch of 'I amness' I am the total complete, 'Poornabrahman' state, the permanent state. The borderline of beingness and non-beingness is intellect-boggling, because the intellect subsides at that precise location. This borderline is the 'maha-yoga'. You must be at that borderline, that 'maha-yoga' state'. You descend into the 'go down' of that state which has the title 'birth'.

When that witness itself, which is 'I am', subsides, what remains? With the witness gone, all other things have disappeared too. By the same token upon the arising of the 'I am', the whole manifestation takes place; these two are not separate, they are one, 'I am' is the witness, the entire manifest world is because of this.

Awareness is primordial; it is the original state, beginningless, endless, uncaused, unsupported, without parts, without change. Consciousness is on contact, a reflection against a surface, a state of duality. There can be no consciousness without awareness, but there can be awareness without consciousness, as in deep sleep. Awareness is absolute, consciousness is relative to its content; consciousness is always of something. Consciousness is partial and changeful, awareness is total, changeless, calm and silent. And it is the common matrix of every experience. Since it is awareness that makes consciousness possible, there is awareness in every state of consciousness. Therefore, the very consciousness of being conscious is already a movement in awareness. Interest in your stream of consciousness takes you to awareness. It is not a new state. It is at once recognized as the original, basic experience, which is life itself, and also love and joy.

Awareness is unattached and unshaken. It is lucid, silent, peaceful, alert and unafraid, without desire and fear. Meditate on it as your true being and try to be it in your daily life, and you shall realize it in its fullness.

Awareness with an object we call witnessing. When there is also self-identification with the object, caused by desire or fear, such a state is called a person. In reality there is only one state; when distorted by self-identification it is called a person, when colored with the sense of being, it is the witness; when colorless and limitless, it is called the Supreme.

At present, you are moved by the pleasure-pain principle which is the ego. You are going along with the ego, you are not fighting it. You are not even aware how totally you are swayed by personal considerations. A man should be always in revolt against himself, for the ego, like a crooked mirror, narrows down and distorts. It is the worst of all the tyrants, it dominates you absolutely.

At the root of everything is the feeling 'I am'. The state of mind 'there is a world' is secondary, for to be, I do not need the world, the world needs me.

When 'I am myself' goes the 'I am all' comes. When the 'I am all' goes, 'I am' comes. When even 'I am' goes, reality alone is, and in it every 'I am' is preserved and glorified.

When 'I am' arises, everything appears; when 'I am' subsides everything subsides. Now this is what I am trying to tell you, but you want something else. You want something about your future, something which is part of manifestation, but I am trying to hit at it.

When desire and fear end, bondage also ends. It is the emotional involvement, the pattern of likes and dislikes which we call character and temperament, that create the bondage. Don't be afraid of freedom from desire and fear. It enables you to live a life so different from all you know, so much more intense and interesting, that truly by losing all you gain all.

When did this process of observing start? It started with the arrival of the waking state, deep sleep state and the knowledge 'I am', all rolled into one 'I am'. This is known as birth. With the so-called birth, this triad has come, and with its arrival observation started. Every day it is going on. The moment the 'I amness' comes it is being used for experiencing, observing etc. Prior to the happening of this birth, where was the 'I amness'? It was not there.

Be alert to the 'I am' and all other experiences will be transcended.

Be aware that whatever happens, happens to you, by you, through you; that you are the creator, enjoyer and destroyer of all you perceive and you will not be afraid. Unafraid, you will not be unhappy, nor will you seek happiness.

When I met my Guru, he told me: 'you are not what you take yourself to be. Find out what you are. Watch the sense 'I am', find you real self' I obeyed him because I trusted him; I did as he told me. All my spare time I would spend looking at myself in silence. And what a difference it made, and how soon. It took me only three years to realize my true nature. My Guru died soon after I met him, but it made no difference. I remembered what he told me and persevered. The fruit of it is here, with me.

When I met my guru, he told me: 'You are not what you take yourself to be. Find out what you are. Watch the sense "I am", find your real self'. I obeyed him, because I trusted him. I did as he told me. All my spare time I would spend looking at myself in silence. And what difference it made, and how soon! It took me only three years to realize my true nature.

Be content with what you are sure of. And the only thing you can be sure of is 'I am'. Stay with it and reject everything else. This is Yoga.

Whatever is observed in the manifest world is your own Self, The observer is 'I am', It is a receptacle of the five elements and three gunas. The entire universe is in activity because of the three gunas. The play of the entire world is based on the five elements and three gunas. But you cling to your body; the body is also a play of the five elements and three gunas.

Whatever may be the situation, if it is acceptable, it is pleasant. If it not acceptable, it is painful. What makes it acceptable is not important; the cause may be physical, or psychological, or untraceable; acceptance is the decisive factor. Obversely, suffering is due to non-acceptance. Why [shouldn't pain be acceptable]? Did you ever try? Do try and you will find in pain a joy which pleasure cannot yield, for the simple reason that acceptance of pain takes you much deeper than pleasure does.

Whatever you observe, you don't require, that principle through which 'you are' is greater. In the waking state 'you are' so you have needs, in the absence of 'I amness' where are the needs? In spite of being, not having the knowledge of being is non-being, that state is a source of peace.

Whatever you presently know is false, if the 'I am' is there, Ishwara is there. The 'I am' is Ishwara's soul and Ishwara is my soul, both exist together. Ishwara is without limits, I am also like that, like Ishwara, penniless. Now, just forget everything and find out how will you be on a permanent basis? All this talk of God and yourself is just for killing time. Go ahead, no God, no I, as long as you have cravings, knowledge will not be yours, Ishwara dies before me.

Whatever you see pertains only to That, to your 'I amness'. Spontaneously 'It is'! You are That principle. Don't try to unravel it with your intellect. Just observe and accept it as it is.

Be one with the knowledge 'I am', the source of sentience, the beingness itself. If you are seeking that peace which is priceless, it can only be in establishing yourself in the consciousness with steadfast conviction. By conviction I mean never doubted, firm, unshakable, never wavering – have that kind of conviction in your beingness. Think of nothing else; pray to nothing else, 'Atma Prem', because of it everything is.

Be that 'I am', once you know who you are, remain stabilized in the experience of the Self. Be like Arjuna, Awareness of his Being remained with him constantly, even when he went into the thick of battle. Because he was with Krishna, he could go into battle, knowing that there is nobody who kills and no one who is killed.

Because of the knowledge 'I am' we conduct all activities. In the morning when you wake up you get the first guaranty, that conviction of 'I am'. Then because you are not in a position to sustain or tolerate that 'I amness' you bestir yourself. You get up and move around here and there and the activity starts.

Because the 'I am' principle is there, it is moving all over. To recognize it, you put on various uniforms in order to give it identity, but the principle is already there, and because of that principle you are engaging in various activities. Unless you wear the uniform (the body) you will not be able to conduct any activities. Once you discard this 'I amness' uniform, what remains is the 'Parabrahman".

Whatever concepts I give blast your concepts. I have presently no abundance of thoughts but only those pertaining to the 'I am'. A common man he feels that his hopes and desires would be fulfilled so life if important to him. After listening to the talks here all hopes and desires are not fulfilled, but you transcend them.

Become free from concepts, no concepts, including the 'I am'. The 'I am' is the primary concept, the primary illusion The primary concept itself, for its sustenance, created so many substances, like wheat flour and wheat products. Out of the touch of 'I amness' arose so many concepts and various names.

Whatever happens, happens to you, by you, through you; you are the creator, enjoyer and destroyer of all you perceive.

Whatever I am telling you, is not the truth, because it has come out of this 'I am'. The truth is beyond expression. I am taking you again and again to the source of the spring. Once you go to the source you will come to know there is no water, water is the news 'I am'.

Whatever is called God or Self is because there is the beingness, the feeling that 'I am'. That is the fundamental principle, the basis of all your knowledge, but you are identifying yourself with the body.

Whatever is created is created by the knowledge 'I am'. Do not pursue this path of running after experiences.

Becoming established in the Awareness 'I am' is all that is important. Later on you also transcend the 'I amness'. Just as a storm is a form created by nature, similarly this 'I am', this chemical, was also created. Forget about what I have told you, because that is also a mechanical thing, a chemical. Just be Aware, and then it won't matter if you die a hundred times.

Before descending into this 'avatar', this knowledge quality was not present; knowingness was not there. The 'I am' was absent, not available. It is a non-knowing state, but afterwards, the state comprises all conceptual titles and names, and they are a person's shackles. Any person, any embodied person with that knowledge 'I am' carries on his activities in the world with shackles of name only.

Before the emanation of any words, 'I' already exist; later I say mentally 'I am'. The word-free and thought-free state is the 'atman'.

What relationship can there be between what is and what merely appears to be? Is there any relationship between the ocean and its waves? The real enables the unreal to appear and causes it to disappear. The succession of transient moments creates the illusion of time, but the timeless reality of pure being is not in movement, for all movement requires a motionless background. It is itself the background. Once you have found it in yourself, you know that you had never lost that independent being, independent of all divisions and separations. But don't look for it in consciousness, you will not find it there. Don't look for it anywhere, for nothing contains it. On the contrary, it contains everything and manifests everything. It is like the daylight that makes everything visible while itself remaining invisible.

What was conceived has grown physically, and some of the expressions of this knowledge 'I am' have achieved tremendous things. At the end of the time span the magnificent personalities, and whatever they have achieved – both have disappeared, however long the time, there is an end to it.

What would be the evidence of your existence?

What you must witness is not your thoughts but the consciousness 'I am'. Everything is an expression of the 'I am,' but you are not that; you are prior to the 'I am'.

Whatever activities happen, happen only because of your 'I amness'. They make no impression on the 'I amness'. Judgments like good or bad are aspects of the mind, but if you are one with that 'I amness', then at that stage the mind is not there.

Before the idea 'I am' sprouted, you are, but you don't know you are. Subsequent to that there have been many happenings with which you have started decorating yourself. You try to derive the meaning of yourself out of subsequent words, happenings, and the meaning of words…that is not you…give it up. You are prior to the idea 'I am'. Camp yourself there, prior to the words 'I am'.

Before this knowledge 'I am' appeared on you, you were absolutely unattached. As soon as this knowledge dawned on you, you became attached to everything around you. Only that false 'I' is attached. Everything is just happening and that false 'I' is taking the credit for doing things.

What is this state before this knowledge 'I am' came upon me? When the knowledge 'I am' came, the one who is satisfied with that will reach the state where he considers himself God and 'Brahman'. But he does not go beyond it or prior to it. In the ultimate state lies the prior state; that is, the state before this knowledge 'I am' ever dawned on me – the highest state, the best state, the original state.

Before you can say 'I am', you must be there to say it. Being need not be self-conscious. You need not know to be, but you must 'be' to know.

Before you occurred to yourself as 'I am'; you were in the highest state – the guru of the gurus – the 'Parabrahman' state. Later on you started filling up with all kinds of grosser matter and you came down to the body sense – I am the body. So, all these impurities have to be removed. Until then, you have to stay put in the quietude.

What is wrong is that you consider yourself to be limited to this body and shape. What knowledge I try to give is given to the knowledge 'I am' in each of you, which is the same. If you try to get the knowledge as an individual you will never get it.

What is your core state? In that true accomplished state, there is no scope for even space, let alone the words. In the process of understanding my Guru's words as to how 'I am' I realized 'I am not'. In that state there is no unstruck sound either. In the process of Neti,Neti (Not this, not this) it happens, in the state of 'I amness' finally everything disappears and you get stabilized. If you realize and stabilize, then even if you are silent people will fall at your feet.

What makes the present so different? Obviously, my presence, I am real for I am always 'now', in the present, and what is with me now shares in my reality. The past is in memory, the future – in imagination. There is nothing in the present event itself that makes it stand out as real. A thing focused in the now is with me, for I am ever present, it is my own reality that I impart to the present event.

Begin with feeling 'I am'. All else is neither true nor false, it seems real when it appears, it disappears when it is denied. A transient thing is a mystery. The real is simple, open, clear and kind, beautiful and joyous. It is completely free of contradictions. It is ever-new, ever-fresh, and endlessly creative. Being and non-being, life and death, all distinctions merge in it.

Beingness (the 'I am'), you realize everything is 'You', it is all your creation.

What prevents you from knowing yourself as all and beyond all, is the mind based on memory. It has power over you as long as you trust it. Don't struggle with it; just disregard it. Deprived of attention, it will slow down and reveal the mechanism of its working. Once you know its nature and purpose, you will not allow it to create imaginary problems. What problems can there be which the mind did not create? Life and death do not create problems; pains and pleasures come and go, experienced and forgotten. It is memory and anticipation that create problems of attainment or avoidance, colored by like and dislike. Beingness can act in the world only with the aid of the body. This body is the quintessence of the five elements, and the quintessence of the body-essence is the knowledge 'I am'. The presiding principle of the whole functioning is the knowledge 'I am'. This knowledge 'I am' has to be correctly understood.

Beingness is the lord of the universe, therefore, all the time, be with the lord of manifestation and all your problems and puzzles will be cleared. This knowledge that 'I am' makes perception possible, make it you own. Whatever you may want, just do this (abide in the 'I am') and you will have everything. In this knowledge 'I am' is the entire universe. Consciousness is the lord of all manifestation, only because of the body that we consider this consciousness as a bodily principle.

Behind faith there is a primary cause, the big cause, which is the knowledge 'I am'. The Awareness of my Being happened automatically, it just happens, the sprouting of the knowledge 'I am' is prior to the formation of the five elements.

What is Ishwara? My Guru told me that the one who is listening is Ishwara itself. The 'I am' is Ishwara, there are various names given to that 'I am' but that 'I am' is not your body. Your knowledge 'I am' contains the whole universe, presently it is difficult for you to believe, so for the moment worship it. Beingness contains everything, worship that and all your requirements will be met. Ultimately the knowledge is yours.

What is it in you that understands this knowledge 'I am' without a name, title or word? Sink in that innermost center and witness the knowledge 'I am'.

What is really your own, you are not conscious of. What you are conscious of is neither you nor yours. Yours is the power of perception, not what you perceive. It is a mistake to take the conscious to be the whole of man. Man is the unconscious, the conscious and the superconscious, but you are not the man. Yours is the cinema screen, the light as well as the seeing power, but the picture is not you.

Between the remembered and the actual there is a basic difference which can be observed from moment to moment. At no point of time is the actual the remembered. Between the two there is a difference in kind, not merely in intensity. The actual is unmistakably so. By no effort of will or imagination can you interchange the two. Now, what is it that gives this unique quality to the actual? A moment back, the remembered was actual, in a moment the actual will be the remembered. What makes the actual unique?

What is religion? A cloud in the sky. I live in the sky, not in the clouds, which are so many words held together. Remove the verbiage and what remains? Truth remains.

What is the most ingrained habit you have? It is to say 'I am'. This is the root habit. Words and experiences are unworthy of you. This habit of experiencing will not go until you realize that all this is the domain of five elements, and the experiences in the five elements, are unreal. This 'I amness' itself is unreal.

What is this knowingness? It is the stamp or registration of the booking 'I am'. You are booking a flat, which is under construction but where is the flat? It is only the booking. Similarly this 'I am' is only booking, it represents your Absolute state.

Brahman means the emanation of the world, simultaneously confirming that 'I am'. In this Brahman everything is illusion, but who understands that? The principle that understands, realizes, and witnesses is the 'Parabrahman'. Witnessing happens to the 'Parabrahman'. In this manifest state everything is ever changing, nothing is permanent, and all is illusion.

Break the bonds of memory and self-identification and the shell [of the person] will break by itself. There is a center that imparts reality to whatever it perceives. All you need is to understand that you are the source of reality, that you give reality instead of getting it, that you need no support and no confirmation. Things are as they are because you accept them as they are. Stop accepting them and they will dissolve. Whatever you think about with desire or fear appears before you as real. Look at it without desire or fear and it does lose substance. Pleasure and pain are momentary. It is simpler and easier to disregard them than to act on them.

What do you mean by study? That means you are only trying to remember the concepts. What I am saying is that you become concept-free. Put an ax to the concepts, including the concept 'I am'.

What else is there except the touch of 'I am'? Why do you worry about discovering Maya and Brahma and all that? Understand what this principle 'I am' is and you are finished. That 'I am' is in bondage because of concepts.

What equipment you are having is that 'prana'. 'Upasana' means worship, worship of 'prana' itself. For doing that what equipment do you possess? It is 'prana' itself. Along with 'prana' there is that knowledge 'I am', or consciousness. These two things are available to you to do anything, nothing more than that.

What exactly is born? What is born are three states: the waking state, the sleep state, and the knowledge 'I am', this consciousness. The body and the vital breath would not be able to function if this consciousness were not present. These three states work through the three attributes ('gunas'). I very clearly see that which has been born. And I also know that I am not that which is born. And that is why I am totally fearless. So this knowledge 'I am', this consciousness, this feeling or sense of being, is the quintessence of the body. And if that body essence is gone, this feeling, the sense of being, will also have gone.

But how can such a state be attained? Only if one totally accepts the knowledge 'I am' as oneself with full conviction and faith and firmly believes in the dictum 'I am that by which I know I am'. This knowledge 'I am' is the 'charan-amrita'. Why is it called 'amrita', the nectar? Because it is said, by drinking nectar one becomes immortal. Thus a true devotee, by abiding in the knowledge 'I am' transcends the experience of death and attains immortality.

But I have already told you, you are Ishwara. You have to have the conviction that 'I am That', a mental determination. With the appearance of the knowledge 'I am', appears the space and the four other elements, your beingness gives rise to them, first beingness, then others When you identify with it and stabilize in the beingness, you are not even that. In the knowledge of the Jnani (or the Absolute), the world is all a spectacle, the Jnani is apart from the knowledge ' I am'.

By chanting 'I am Brahman' you become subtle and escape the sense of body and mind. You must accept that you are without a body-mind and that you are subtle. That sense must be instilled in you. I took to this Brahma state, my Beingness or 'I amness' and observe my body.

Watch your thoughts as you watch the street traffic. People come and go; you register without response. It may not be easy in the beginning, but with some practice you will find that your mind can function on many levels at the same time and you can be aware of them all. It is only when you have a vested interest in any particular level that your attention gets caught in it and you black out on other levels.

Watch yourself closely and you will see that whatever be the content of consciousness, the witnessing of it does not depend on the content. Awareness is itself and does not change with the event. The event may be pleasant or unpleasant, minor or important, awareness is the same. Take note of the peculiar nature of pure awareness, its natural self-identity, without the least trace of self-consciousness, and go to the root of it and you will soon realize that awareness is your true nature, and nothing you may be aware of, you can call your own. When the content is viewed without likes and dislikes, the consciousness of it is awareness. But still there is a difference between awareness as reflected in consciousness and pure awareness beyond consciousness. Reflected awareness, the sense "I am aware" is the witness, while pure awareness is the essence of reality. Reflection of the sun in a drop of water is a reflection of the sun, no doubt, but not the sun itself.

What do you mean by 'I am' or the feeling of 'you are'? All the names relate to the 'I amness', Atman also is its name. If there is no 'I amness', whose names can these all be? You cannot say this and that consciousness, your consciousness is your world only. To fully understand and realize all this, do meditation. That sound, the humming 'I am', is the Ishwara sound. It is a reminder that, you are God, but your reject the soundless sound by identifying with the body. On your own authority, in absence of the 'I am' principle, what can you do?

By focusing the mind on 'I am', on the sense of being, 'I am so and-so' dissolves; 'am a witness only' remains and that too submerges in 'I am all'. Then the all becomes the One and the One – yourself, not to be separate from me. Abandon the idea of a separate 'I' and the question of 'whose experience?' will not arise. On a deeper level my experience is your experience. Dive deep within yourself and you will find it easily and simply. Go in the direction of 'I am'.

We love variety, the play of pain and pleasure, we are fascinated by contrasts. For this we need the opposites and their apparent separation. We enjoy them for a time and then get tired and crave for the peace and silence of pure being.

What capital is available to you? Only the 'I am', it is a product of this five-elemental food essence. First you become the consciousness, and then you realize that you are the manifestation.

What changes is not real, what is real does not change. Now, what is it in you that does not change? As long as there is food, there is body and mind. When the food is stopped, the body dies and the mind dissolves. But does the observer perish? It is a matter of actual experience that the self has being independent of mind and body. It is being-awareness-bliss. Awareness of being is bliss.

By its very nature, the mind is outward turned; it always tends to seek for the source of things among the things themselves; to be told to look for the source within, is, in a way, the beginning of a new life. Awareness takes the place of consciousness; in consciousness there is the "I", who is conscious, while awareness is undivided; awareness is aware of itself. The "I am" is a thought, while awareness is not a thought; there is no "I am aware" in awareness. Consciousness is an attribute while awareness is not; one can be aware of being conscious, but not conscious of awareness. God is the totality of consciousness, but awareness is beyond all - being as well as not-being.

Until that voice ('I am') of consciousness came, I was not concerned. Once it left, I went too, so be with the consciousness (the 'I am'), all the teachings are based on this. This concern for the world is because of consciousness; it will be there as long as consciousness is there.

By meditating on the knowledge 'I am' it gradually settles down at its source and disappears, then you are the Absolute.

Until you are free of the drug [of self-identification], all your religions and sciences, prayers and yogas are of no use to you, for, based on a mistake, they strengthen it.

By reading various books and listening to everything else, you cannot become a 'mahatma', but only through that knowledge 'I am'. Don't concentrate on the body; because of a body you call yourself male or female. Just hold on to that knowledge 'I am' only without body sense – beyond name and form or design. But you have to employ name, form and design for the sake of worldly activities.

Until you recognize and completely identify yourself with the knowledge 'I am', you will identify with the body. When one disidentifies with the body, one transcends not only the body but consciousness as well, since consciousness is a product of the body. The consciousness no longer says 'I am', 'I am'.

Was it not the sense of 'I am' that came first? Some seed consciousness must be existing even during sleep, or swoon. On waking up the experience runs: 'I am-the body- in the world'. It may appear to arise in succession but in fact it is all simultaneous, a single idea of having a body in a world. Can there be the sense of 'I am' without being somebody or other?

Was there ever a world without troubles? Your being as a person depends on violence to others. Your very body is a battlefield, full of the dead and dying. Existence implies violence. There is little of non-violence in nature. Do you realize that, as long as you have a self to defend, you must be violent?

By staying in this knowledge ('I am') you can dissolve the subtle body. The pill – the three states (waking, sleep and beingness) – dissolves. Then there is no coming, till then the subtle body will remain. So long the food essence is there the 'I am' knowledge is there, once the essence is exhausted, knowingness goes.

Catch hold of that 'I am' only and all obstacles will evaporate. If you correctly understand me, you will be beyond the realm of body-mind. Many a times it happens that teachings are misunderstood. Because the 'I am' is there, these questions arise, If the 'I am' is not there, no questions can arise. In the realm of 'I am' anything is possible, but if I were alert enough, do you think I would have been in this body? The Jnani is the one who knows that beingness, the world and Brahman are unreal. Having understood the 'I am', I transcend it and came to the conclusion that all the three entities are unreal, and then what more remains to be liquidated? The 'Parabrahman' is without attributes.

Catch hold of the 'I am' and all obstacles will evaporate, you will be beyond the realm of body-mind.

Catch hold of the knowledge 'I am' in meditation and the realization will occur that 'I', the Absolute, am not the quality 'I am'.

Can any of your concepts grasp the total, the Ultimate? Have you understood that knowledge itself is ignorance? If it were real it would have been there eternally – it would not have had a beginning and an end. Now the experience 'I am' is felt, earlier that experience was not. When it was not, no proof was called for, but once it is, lots of proof is required.

Unless you know yourself well, how can you know another? And when you know yourself, you are the other.

Understand that the knowledge 'I am' has dawned on you and all are its manifestations, in this understanding you realize you are not the 'I am'.

Understanding the 'I am', your sense of 'being' or just 'presence' is extremely important as on it rests the entire outcome of the teaching.

Understanding what that 'avatar' is, Lord Krishna avatar means in essence abiding in that only. Then one is not the body. And what is the body? It is a mere aid for the sustenance or endurance of that 'I am' principle.

Unless you have the understanding of 'I amness', there is no progress. Once you understand the 'I am', there is nothing further to understand. When your 'I amness' is gone, together with everything, then there is nothing. Then that Nothingness is everything, but there no one left to say so.

Cling to the one thing that matters, hold on to 'I am' and let go all else. This is 'sadhana'. In realization there is nothing to hold on to and nothing to forget. Everything is known, nothing is remembered.

Concepts come into the sense of being 'I am' because of the vital breath that causes the mind flow. Mind means words, so thoughts are there – they are the concepts. Look at your root, the child consciousness, and finish it off.

True awareness (samvid) is a state of pure witnessing, without the least attempt to do anything about the event witnessed. Your thoughts and feelings, words and actions may also be a part of the event; you watch all unconcerned, in the full light of clarity and understanding. You understand precisely what is going on, because it does not affect you. It may seem to be an attitude of cold aloofness, but it is not really so. Once you are in it, you will find that you love what you see, whatever may be its nature. This choiceless love is the touchstone of awareness. If it is not there, you are merely interested, for some personal reasons.

Concern yourself with your mind, remove its distortions and impurities. Once you had the taste of your own self, you will find it everywhere and at all times. Therefore it is so important that you should come to it. Once you know it, you will never lose it.

Consciousness and life - both you may call God; but you are beyond both, beyond God, beyond being and not-being.

Ultimately all these concepts can and must be understood to be false, but the difficulty and the essential thing is to be convinced that the original basic concept 'I am' itself is false.

Ultimately one must go beyond knowledge, but the knowledge must come, and knowledge can come by constant meditation. By meditating, the knowledge 'I am' gradually settles down and merges with universal knowledge, and thereby becomes totally free, like the sky or the space. It is not possible for you to acquire knowledge, you 'are' knowledge. You are what you are seeking.

Trust the teacher. Take my case. My Guru ordered me to attend to the sense 'I am' and to give attention to nothing else. I just obeyed. I did not follow any particular course of breathing or meditation, or study of scriptures. Whatever happened I would turn away my attention from it and remain with the sense 'I am', it may look too simple, even crude. My only reason for doing it was that my Guru told me so. Yet it worked! Obedience is a powerful solvent of all desires and fears. Understand that it is not the individual that has consciousness; it is the consciousness which assumes innumerable forms. That something which is born or which will die is purely imaginary. It is the child of a barren woman. In the absence of this basic concept 'I am', there is no thought, there is no consciousness.

Consciousness creates everything. All greatness is because of the 'I am'. There is no other path, only this conviction. This is it!

Consciousness is always of movement, of change. There can be no such thing a changeless consciousness. Changelessness wipes out consciousness immediately. A man deprived of outer or inner sensations blanks out, or goes into the birthless and deathless state. Only when spirit and matter come together, consciousness is born.

Consciousness is the sense of knowingness 'I am' without words, and it appeared unknowingly and unsolicited. Only in the realm of knowingness 'I am' – the consciousness – can a world be, and so also an experience. Hold on to this knowingness 'I am' and the fount of knowledge will well up within you, revealing the mystery of the Universe; of your body and psyche; of the play of the five elements, the three 'gunas' and 'prakriti-purusha'; and of everything else. In the process of this revelation, your individualistic personality confined to the body shall expand into the manifested universe, and it will be realized that you permeate and embrace the entire cosmos as your 'body' only. This is known as the 'Pure Super-knowledge' – 'Shuddhavijnana'.

Consciousness or 'Ishwara' is not that of an individual. 'Ishwara' means the expression of all forms. This chemical, this ingredient, is your 'I amness' and it is sustained by consuming the food body.

To see myself in everybody, and everybody in myself, most certainly is love.

To see reality is as simple as to see one's face in a mirror. Only the mirror must be clear and true. A quiet mind, undistorted by desires and fears, free from ideas and opinions, clear on all the levels, is needed to reflect the reality. Be clear and quiet, alert and detached, all else will happen by itself.

Totally accept the knowledge 'I am' as oneself, and with full conviction and faith firmly believe in the dictum 'I am that by which I know I am'.

To start with you have to be in that beingness or 'I am' without the body sense. You feel that you are the body now but when you abide in that beingness you will know then how you are without the body sense. But don't forget, at the same time; that body and the vital breath are very necessary. Once you understand these three entities correctly (body, vital breath and the message 'I am'), then you are apart.

To understand more clearly take the example of the dream world. You are in deep sleep and suddenly you feel 'I am' and that 'I amness' creates a dream world. Similarly this manifest world is created by that 'I amness'. You will realize this later in the search for truth. The last progress will be for you to transcend this 'I amness' and get stabilized in the ultimate.

Conviction! That is the only technique for the 'sadhana', if you are thinking of any initiation…only the words of the guru that you are not the body! That is the initiation. Stay put there, in that state. It is spontaneous, natural, that 'shraddha' (faith). What is that faith? 'I am' without words, whatever you are that is the faith. Now you have to elevate yourself to the state of 'Brahman'; this is the condition you have to develop.

Day by day your conviction that the knowledge. 'I am' is God must grow. Don't care about the body, by constant meditation, when God is pleased, you will have complete knowledge in the realm of Consciousness. You may go anywhere, but don't forget that the knowledge, 'I am' itself is God.

Deal with the knowledge 'I am'. This 'I amness' is there first, isn't it? – Primary. That 'I' must be there before you receive this sickness of 'samskara' (obstacles). Initially you have to understand that the knowledge 'I am' is a product of the food essence. When you know that you are, the world also is.

Death is considered to be a traumatic experience, but understand what happens. That which has been born, the knowledge 'I am', will end. That knowledge, which was limited by this body, will then become unlimited, so what is to be feared?

To know what you are you must first investigate and know what you are not. And to know what you are not, you must watch yourself carefully, rejecting all that does not necessarily go with basic fact 'I am'. The ideas: I am born at a given place, at a given time, from my parents and now I am so-and-so, living at, married to, father of, employed by, and so on, are not inherent in the sense 'I am'. Our usual attitude is 'I am this' or 'that'. Separate consistently and perseveringly the 'I am' from 'this' or 'that' and try to feel what it means to be, just to 'be', without being 'this' or 'that'. All our habits go against it and the task of fighting them is long and hard sometimes, but clear understanding helps a lot. The clearer you understand that on the level of the mind you can be described in negative terms only, the quicker you will come to the end of your search and realize your limitless being.

To know that you are neither body nor mind, watch yourself steadily and live unaffected by your body and mind, completely aloof, as if you were dead. It means you have no vested interests, either in the body or in the mind. Just remain unaffected. This complete aloofness, unconcern with mind and body is the best proof that at the core of your being you are neither mind nor body. What happens to the body and the mind may not be within your power to change, but you can always put an end to your imagining yourself to be body and mind. Whatever happens, remind yourself that only your body and mind are affected, not yourself.

To know the self as the only reality and all else as temporal and transient is freedom, peace and joy. It is all very simple. Instead of seeing things as imagined, learn to see them as they are. When you can see everything as it is, you will also see yourself as you are. It is like cleansing a mirror. The same mirror that shows you the world as it is will also show you your own face. The thought 'I am' is the polishing cloth. Use it.

To know these senses, to understand these secrets, you surrender to that very principle 'I am', and that consciousness alone will lead you to this. Presently stabilize in the consciousness. If you don't do that, your very concepts will be very dangerous to you – they will throttle you to death. The knowledge you are, is the very source of all energy, the source of all Gods, of all types of knowledge. This is the simplest method, you know you are, just be there.

Delve deeply into the sense 'I am' and you surely discover that the perceiving center is universal, as universal as the light that illumines the world. All that happens in the universe happens to you, the silent witness. On the other hand, whatever is done, is done by you, the universal and inexhaustible energy.

Develop the witness attitude and you will find in your own experience that detachment brings control. The state of witnessing is full of power, there is nothing passive about it.

To produce the source of the mind, 'I am', you must have the ingredient of the five-elemental juice. If that is available, the sprouting of the mind can begin with 'I am'. You know you are before even speaking the words 'I am'. Subsequent to the knowingness 'I am', you say 'I am' by words.

Did you ever see the moon and all before the appearance of the beingness, Brahma or this illusion? Although the 'I am' is ample and plenty, it is an illusion that induces multiplicity. This manifest world is a dynamic play of the five elements and there is no scope for an individual. Just as a diamond radiates from all sides, similarly in deep meditation you will realize that you are this entire manifestation.

To establish oneself firmly in the awareness 'I am', it is not necessary to think 'I am', 'I am'. Is it necessary to think you are sitting here? You know that you are sitting here. Whatever name and form there is belongs to that material and that material is not you. Do you analyze the problem and with the firm conviction decide that you are not the material? When the material disintegrates what does the name refer to? Does it have any significance? Only one in ten million goes to the crux of the matter, analyzes what it is, comes to a conclusion, and gets liberated, all by himself. The one who gets liberated is the consciousness, there is no entity.

Discard all you are not and go ever deeper. Just as a man digging a well discards what is not water, until he reaches the water-bearing strata, so must you discard what is not your own, till nothing is left which you can disown. You will find that what is left is nothing which the mind can hook on to. You are not even a human being. You just are - a point of awareness, co-extensive with time and space and beyond both, the ultimate cause, itself uncaused. If you ask me "Who are you?", my answer would be: "Nothing in particular. Yet, I am."

Discover all you are not. Body, feelings, thoughts, ideas, time, space, being and not-being this or that -nothing concrete or abstract you can point out to is you. A mere verbal statement will not do -you may repeat a formula endlessly without any result whatsoever. You must watch yourself continuously -particularly your mind - moment by moment, missing nothing. This witnessing is essential for the separation of the self from the not-self.

To abide in the knowledge 'I am' is one's true religion – the 'svadharma'. But instead of following it, you opted to be irreligious by submitting to the dictates of your concepts, which led you to believe that you are a body. This misconception ensured only the fear of death.

To be a living being is not the ultimate state; there is something beyond, much more wonderful, which is neither being nor non-being, neither living nor not-living. It is a state of pure awareness, beyond the limitations of space and time. Once the illusion that the body-mind is oneself is abandoned, death loses its terror, it becomes a part of living.

To be the point of light (reflected as the sense 'I am') tracing the world is 'turiya'. To be the light itself is 'turiyatita'. But of what use are names when reality is so near?

Discrimination is very necessary to understand what I am saying. It is only after the arrival of consciousness that we try to understand ourselves. Consciousness is the so-called birth, birth means the three aspects: waking state, deep sleep and the knowledge 'I am'. Once I understand what this birth is, then the whole mystery is solved. Since I have thoroughly known what this birth principle is, I will know very well at that happening of so-called death. I shall observe the departure of the vital breath, the language and the 'I amness", there is no question of death.

To be, you must be nobody. To think yourself to be something, or somebody, is death and hell.

To do away with body-mind sense or identity, imbibe or dwell in the 'I am'. Later the 'I am' will merge into the ultimate nature.

Do not bother about anything you want, or think, or do, just stay put in the thought and feeling, 'I am', focusing 'I am' firmly in your mind. All kinds of experience may come to you – remain unmoved in the knowledge that all perceivable is transient and only the 'I am' endures.

This primary concept, 'I amness' is dishonest, because it is still a concept only. Finally one has to transcend that also and be in the 'nirvikalpa' state, which means the concept-free state. Then you have no concept at all, not even of 'I am'. In that state one does not know that one is. This state is known as 'Parabrahman': 'Brahman' transcended. 'Brahman' is manifest; 'Parabrahman' is beyond that, prior to that; the Absolute. Do you understand what I am driving at? Whatever you caught in your attention, that attention should eventually turn into no-attention. The state that is finally left over is Awareness, 'Parabrahman'.

Tirelessly I draw your attention to the one incontrovertible factor – that of being. Being needs no proofs – it proves itself. If only you go deep into the fact of being and discover the vastness and the glory, to which the 'I am' is the door, and cross the door and go beyond, your life will be full of happiness and light. Believe me; the effort needed is as nothing when compared with the discoveries arrived at.

This reality is so concrete, so actual, so much more tangible than mind and matter, that compared to it even diamond is soft like butter. This overwhelming actuality makes the world dreamlike, misty, irrelevant.

This sense of 'being' or the feeling 'I am', was it not the very first event or happening before any of your living experiences could begin?

Do nothing but stay in the knowledge 'I am', the 'moolmaya' or primary illusion, and then it will release its stranglehold on you and get lost.

Do nothing, absolutely nothing! Just be, be the knowledge 'I am' only and abide there. To imbibe this, meditate on beingness only. Catch hold of the knowledge 'I am' in meditation. In this process, the realization occurs that 'I' the Absolute am not the 'guna' 'I am'; therefore in meditation nothing is to be retained in memory. Nevertheless something will appear on the memory screen, but be unconcerned, just be, do nothing. Refrain from grasping anything in meditation; the moment you do, otherness begins, and so does duality. Nothing is to be done. Then all your riddles will be solved and dissolved. 'Moolmaya' – that is, the primary illusion – will release her stranglehold on you and will get lost.

This true knowledge, the knowledge 'I am', is also rendered the status of 'non-knowledge' in the final Absolute state. When one is established in this final free state, the knowledge 'I am' becomes 'non-knowledge'.

Don't get involved in anything, stay in the consciousness 'I am' and don't go on an intellectual binge again. Consciousness indicates to the consciousness, expounds the knowledge; but you will not dwell there, you embrace the body. The knowledge 'I am' tells the knowledge about itself to the 'I am' only.

Don't roam about, don't come here either. Abide in the quietude, peace, stability. Here we are not engaged in any buying or selling. That knowledge 'I am', without concepts, is evoked or stimulated by the consciousness and peace which emanate from this place.

This knowledge of 'I am' spontaneously appeared, it is prior to the formation of the five elements. The Absolute (Paramatman, Parameshwar) is not aware of anything. The state of Awareness comes later, with knowledge of the 'I am'. The Absolute has no knowledge that 'it was' (or that 'it is').

This knowledge of 'I amness' that is there in you contains the whole universe. The knowledge that I am expounding is to that divinity within you (the 'I am') and not to a human being. The 'I amness' which having created the universe is dwelling within you as the remnant. The very core of that knowledge 'You are' contains the whole universe.

This little container of food essence is being sucked by that beingness, 'I am' day and night. The principle that sucks that container is not the body; it is apart from the body. This beingness principle dwells in that food body itself. Just as the child sucks on the mother's breast, the beingness consumes the body.

Don't you see that it is your very search for happiness that makes you feel miserable? Try the other way: indifferent to pain and pleasure, neither seeking, nor refusing, give all your attention to the level on which 'I am' is timelessly present. Soon you will realize that peace and happiness are in your very nature and it is only seeking them through some particular channels that disturbs. Avoid the disturbance, that is all. To seek there is no need; you would not seek what you already have. You yourself are God, the Supreme Reality. To begin with, trust me, trust the teacher. It enables you to make the first step - and then your trust is justified by your own experience.

This passing show maybe likened to the following situation: suppose I was well all along, then suddenly I was sick and the doctor gave me medicine. After three days my fever was gone. So this stage of fever for three days is the 'I am' consciousness.

This primary concept is the knowledge 'I am', it is the mother of all other concepts. In order to get that satisfaction, you must find the source of this primary concept 'I am'. You should give attention to the knowledge 'I am' and meditate on that itself. Knowledge is to be got hold of knowledge only. This will produce the seed, which, through this process of meditation, slowly grows into a big tree, and that itself will give you all the knowledge. It will not be necessary for you to ask anyone what is what.

Don't talk of means, there are no means. What you see as false, dissolves. It is the very nature of illusion to dissolve on investigation. Investigate - that is all. You cannot destroy the false, for you are creating it all the time. Withdraw from it, ignore it, go beyond, and it will cease to be.

Don't you see that it is your very search for happiness that makes you feel miserable? Try the other way: indifferent to pain and pleasure, neither asking nor refusing, give all your attention to the level on which "I am" is timelessly present. Soon you will realize that peace and happiness are in your very nature and it is only seeking them through some particular channels that disturbs. Avoid the disturbance, that is all.

This knowledge ('I am') is for each man to understanding and be still in it. By understanding the Self you understand the world, what else is there? You are as large as the world, if you are; the world is, otherwise not. The trap of birth and death is because of the 'I am', dwell on it, realize it and transcend it.

This knowledge 'I am' comes to you after your body is born, after that the body of childhood grows on its own and becomes old. What remains in the end is only one thing 'I am'. So all through life you have to remember to investigate who is this 'I am'. Otherwise birth and death will have no meaning for your beingness, because that beingness will also be dissolved after the death of the body.

Dwell on the principle ('I am') of that state for a sufficiently long time. All the greatness, significance and magnificence of the entire world is dwelling in the principle 'you are' and 'I am'. That is the prop and that itself is the greatness. There is no other remedy, no other path, except implicit faith and conviction in the Self.

This knowledge 'I am' has appeared out of love and that love comes out of existence. When this knowledge has dawned on the

This knowledge 'I am' has dawned on you, since then whatever other knowledge you have acquired, whatever experiences you have had, whatever you have seen of the world, has all been witnessed. But that one to whom the witnessing takes place is entirely separate from that which is witnessed.

This knowledge 'I am' has spontaneously 'appeared' on your Absolute state, therefore it is an illusion. The feeling 'I am' is itself an illusion, therefore whatever is seen through this illusion cannot be real.

This knowledge 'I am', this consciousness, has come out of the prior state when there was no consciousness. The consciousness is a state which is now with us and because of which we suffer; and before this consciousness came, a state prevailed when we were not conscious and which was a happy state.

This knowledge is ancient ('Sanatana'), it has come from Eternity. From the eternal Absolute, which is ever there, a seed appears, that seed is the 'I amness'. It appears spontaneously, its remnant is in us. This little seed ('I am') sprouts and the whole world is created.

Each of must say 'I am' and realize it. There is no 'you', and there is no 'me', as individual entities. Until the 'I am' thought was there, there was no manifestation; both came about simultaneously.

Earnestness, not perfection, is a precondition to self-realization. Virtues and powers come with realization, not before.

This illness that I have got is not separate from what exists as the body, breath and the knowledge 'I am'. This is one bundle, which has been created; whatever happens is contained in that bundle. I have been separate from it before conception, and will continue to be separate from what has been created.

Establish yourself firmly in the 'I am' and reject all that does not go with it.

This is a subtle point, so try to understand it clearly. When I say 'I was not' prior to conception, then what I actually mean is that I was not like this present 'I am'. But that 'I' which could discern this must be there to judge the absence of the present 'I am'.

This is no joke, but you can become 'Parabrahman' right now. Only it is not a commodity that you can acquire. You, a hundred years ago, were the 'Parabrahman'. Give me all the information about that state of a hundred years back. Focus your attention only on that consciousness 'I am'. Don't be led astray by all the so-called spiritual disciplines and rigmaroles.

This is the greatest miracle, that I got the news 'I am', have you any doubts that you are? It is self-evident. Prior to knowing that you are, what knowledge did you have? 'Dhyana' means to have an objective. You want to consider something. You 'are' that something, just to be, you are. Just being the being 'I am'. You meditate on something; that knowledge 'I am' is yourself. Abide only there. How can you ask any questions at this point? Because, that is, the beginning of knowledge.

Even faith in God is only a stage on the way. Ultimately, you abandon all, for you come to something so simple that there are no words to express it.

Even if you are quite ignorant of the ways and the means, keep quiet and look within; guidance is sure to come. You are never left without knowing what your next step should be. The trouble is that you may shirk it. The guru is there for giving you courage because of his experience and success. But only what you discover through you own awareness, your own effort, will be of permanent use to you.

This is to be understood and realized that the 'I am' is even before the arising of any words and questions in me. People always want a name or concept to indicate the state of 'I am' prior to words. When this is done by giving it a name, like for example Brahman, they feel satisfied.

Even to talk of re-uniting the person with the self is not right, because there is no person, only a mental picture given a false reality by conviction. Nothing was divided and there is nothing to unite.

Every existence is my existence, every consciousness is my consciousness, every sorrow is my sorrow and every joy is my joy - this is universal life. Yet, my real being, and yours too, is beyond the universe and, therefore, beyond the categories of the particular and the universal. It is what it is, totally self-contained and independent.

Everyone, from plants to creatures, want and know the 'I am' to be there, once we have existence, we want it to continue. Your experience is because of the beingness, the world depends on beingness, is it happy or miserable? When your beingness is not there, is it happy or miserable?

Everything is a play of ideas. In the state free from ideation (nirvikalpa samadhi) nothing is perceived. The root idea is 'I am'. It shatters the state of pure consciousness and is followed by the innumerable sensations and perceptions, feelings and ideas, which in their totality constitute God and His world. The 'I am' remains as the witness, but it is by the will of God that everything happens.

This body is like an instrument that says 'I am', like an announcer. Presently you think you are the body-mind, and whatever concepts you have gathered are flowing out. When you begin spirituality, you reject the body-mind with 'I am not that'. Then you come to the 'I am' only, without words. Then you are everything; you are not confined to the body.

This body is only the food body for the consumption and the sustenance of the 'I amness'. You have to remain in that Beingness or Consciousness with firm faith while having no identification with the body or the personality, or with name and form. Always identify yourself with Consciousness, it will take a while for this conviction to root, but persist.

This body packet of the five elements gets conditioned into the ego or individuality. When you transcend the body you dwell in the 'I am' (in manifestation), at that stage you know that all is the five elemental play. So long as the 'I amness' prevails or the 'I am' is realized it is also realized that there is another Absolute principal to which witnessing happens, and That Absolute principal is beyond time.

Experience, however sublime, is not the real thing. By its very nature it comes and goes. Self-realization is not an acquisition. It is more of the nature of understanding. Once arrived at, it cannot be lost. On the other hand, consciousness is changeful, flowing, undergoing transformation from moment to moment. Do not hold on to consciousness and its contents. Consciousness held, ceases. To try to perpetuate a flash of insight, or a burst of happiness is destructive of what it wants to preserve. What comes must go. The permanent is beyond all comings and goings. Go to the root of all experience, to the sense of being. Beyond being and not-being lies the immensity of the real. Try and try again.

This conviction can be strengthened by meditation, 'dhyana'. And 'dhyana' means the knowledge must remain in meditation with the knowledge. Now, what is meditation? Meditation is the knowledge 'I am' remaining in that knowledge. There is the waking state and the sleep state, and the knowledge that you are, I exist, and I know that I exist. Other than that what capital does anyone have than merely knowledge 'I am'? 'Dhyana' is when this knowledge, this consciousness that I am, meditates on itself and not on something other than itself.

Fearlessness comes by itself, when you see that there is nothing to be afraid of. When you walk in a crowded street, you just bypass people. Some you see, some you just glance at, but you do not stop. It is the stopping that creates the bottleneck. Keep moving! Disregard names and shapes, don't be attached to them; your attachment is your bondage.

Find out why you are, what is the cause of your being 'I am'? Actually you had no knowledge that you are or you were. But at this moment, you know you are. Why is that? Understand its cause. You alone know why you are; why is it offered to you that you are, you alone know. Don't ask anyone else about it, but inquire by yourself. Don't bother about others, worry only about yourself. That knowledge 'I am' is the product of what, is due to what? How and why? Inquire only into this matter.

Find out, are you separate unknowingly?

First know your own mind and you will find that the question of other minds does not arise at all, for there are no other people. You are the common factor, the only link between the minds, Being is consciousness; 'I am' applies to all.

First of all, abandon all self-identification, stop thinking of yourself as such-and-such, so-and-so, this or that. Abandon all self-concern, worry not about your welfare, material or spiritual. Abandon any desire, gross or subtle, stop thinking of achievement of any kind. You are complete here and now, you need absolutely nothing.

This 'I am' concept was not there prior to what you call 'birth'. So as this concept has appeared, it will also go away. How am I affected? In no way whatsoever, because it is not true. This applies to all concepts. Prior to birth and after birth, whatever knowledge I have, my own, without hearing it from any one, that is the only true knowledge I accept. And the proof lies in my guru's words.

This 'I am' is a concept also, is it not? And you want to hang on to this concept also. This 'I amness' is not going to remain in your association, and when it goes, everything relating to that 'I amness' goes. When this is the state of affairs, what is the use of trying to gain or assimilate knowledge? You are standing on a concept 'I am' and trying to paint that with another concept.

This 'I am' is an announcement, it is not the real, it has come out of something else. What the real is, I am not trying to tell you, because words negate that. Whatever I am telling you, is not the truth, because it has come out of the 'I am'.

This 'I am' is still there with you, ever present, ever available, it was and still is the first thought, refuse all other thoughts and come back there and stay there.

This 'I amness' quality is the Sattva guna (food essence quality). I am The Absolute, I am not that touch of 'I amness', so long 'I am' is there witnessing will happen to The Absolute spontaneously. The dawn and sunlight depend on time, but their observer does not depend on time.

First of all, establish a constant contact with yourself, be with yourself all the time. Into self-awareness all blessings flow. Begin as a center of observation, deliberate cognizance, and grow into a center of love in action. "I am" is a tiny seed which will grow into a mighty tree - quite naturally, without a trace of effort.

There is trouble only when you cling to something. When you hold on to nothing, no trouble arises. The relinquishing of the lesser is the gaining of the greater. Give up all and you gain all. Then life becomes what it was meant to be: pure radiation from an inexhaustible source. In that light the world appears dimly like a dream.

First there was no message 'I am' and also there was no world. Instantly, the message 'I am' and this magnificent world materialized out of 'nothingness'! How amazing! This message 'I am' is nothing other that the advertisement of the Eternal Truth.

First there was the desire to 'Be'. From this 'I am' the air came first and the earth last. Then from earth came the vegetation and many forms of life, each having this 'I amness'. Because of the five elements you have the body and in that body is the 'I amness'.

There must be love in the relation between the person who says 'I am' and the observer of the 'I am'. As long as the observer, the inner self; the 'higher' self considers himself apart from the observed, the 'lower' self, despises it and condemns it, the situation is hopeless. It is only when the observer ('vyakta') accepts the person ('vyakti') as a projection or manifestation of himself, and so to say, takes the self into the Self, the duality of 'I' and 'this' goes and the identity of the outer and the inner, the Supreme Reality manifests itself.

First you create a world, then the 'I am' becomes a person, who is not happy for various reasons. He goes out in search of happiness, meets a Guru who tells him 'You are not a person, find out who you are'. He does it and goes beyond.

First you have what is called 'atma-bhava' – that is the 'I am' sense. Later, this sense identifies with the form of a body, when it is called 'aham-akar', the 'I am' form, this is ego. Ego is never a title or name, but just a sense of 'I am' prior to words. The waking state, the sleep state and the knowingness 'I am' constitute an ego.

These questions arise because of the conditioning of egoism. When you are in the 'I amness', there is no egoism – it is completely liquidated. Consciousness appears, is seen and then again is gone. It is like air in the sky. The mistake happens because we consider 'That' Consciousness to be the individual consciousness.

These two entities are available to you, the vital force and the knowledge 'I am', the consciousness. They appear without any effort; they are there. Now, in order to be one with 'Ishwara', to understand the non-duality you must worship the vital force. Then that knowledge, which is in seed form, slowly grows. And the seeker becomes full of knowledge; in the process he transcends that, and the ultimate state is achieved.

This 'gun-gun' (humming) is within the knowledge 'I am', which includes the physical form. The 'gun-gun' entity and the knowledge 'I am' and the physical form – that whole bundle – has been created out of the five elements. So up to this point, the whole thing can be said to be entirely mechanistic and therefore pure ignorance.

First, the knowingness knows itself, knowing that 'I am'. And in the illumination by that 'I amness', or that consciousness, everything else is observed. I have had to repeat the same thing again and again, and I do not want to run kindergarten classes of spirituality.

For all beings it is the same experience. Early morning, immediately after waking, just the feeling 'I am' is felt inside or the beingness happens, and therefore further witnessing of all else happens. The first witnessing is that of 'I am', this primary witnessing is the prerequisite for all further witnessing. But to whom is the witnessing occurring? One that ever is, even without waking, to that ever-present substratum the witnessing of the waking state happens.

For meditation you should sit with identification with the knowledge 'I am' only and have confirmed to yourself that you are not the body. You must dwell only in that knowledge 'I am' – not merely the words 'I am'. And the indwelling knowledge that you are, without words, that itself you are. In that identity you must stabilize yourself. And then whatever doubts you have will be cleared by that very knowledge, and everything will be opened up to you.

For reality to be, the ideas of "me" and "mine" must go. They will go if you let them. Then your normal natural state reappears, in which you are neither the body nor the mind, neither the "me" nor the "mine", but in a different state of being altogether. It is pure awareness of being, without being this or that, without any self-identification with anything in particular or in general. In that pure light of consciousness there is nothing, not even the idea of nothing. There is only light.

Freedom comes through renunciation. All possession is bondage. If you do not have the wisdom and the strength to give up, just look at your possessions. Your mere looking will burn them up. If you can stand outside your mind, you will soon find that total renunciation of possessions and desires is the most obviously reasonable thing to do. You create the world and then worry about it. Becoming selfish makes you weak. If you think you have the strength and courage to desire, it is because you are young and inexperienced. Invariably the object of desire destroys the means of acquiring it and then itself withers away. It is all for the best, because it teaches you to shun desire like poison. No need of any acts of renunciation. Just turn your mind away, that is all. Desire is merely the fixation of the mind on an idea. Get it out of its grove by denying it attention. Whatever may be the desire or fear, don't dwell upon it. Here and there you may forget, it does not matter. Go back to your attempts till the brushing away of every desire and fear, of every reaction, becomes automatic.

There is that nine-month period in the womb. So what is the content of the womb? It is that knowledge 'I am' in dormant condition. This is being developed slowly, so within the birth principle everything is contained. That which is called birth, the birth principle is 'turiya'; the experience that you exist itself is 'turiya'. 'Turiya' means where the consciousness is. One who knows 'turiya' is 'turiyatita'. That is my state. 'Turiya' is within the consciousness, which is the product of the five elements. And one who transcends that, who knows the 'turiya', is 'turiyatita'. In order to stabilize in 'turiya', you must know the birth principle. 'Turiya' is always described as the witness state that sees through waking, dreaming and sleeping. And 'turiyatita' is even beyond that.

For this [self-realization], you need a well-ordered and quiet life, peace of mind and immense earnestness.

Forget all about physical disciplines in this connection and just be with the knowledge 'I am'. When you are established in the 'I am' there are no thoughts or words.

Freedom from all desire is eternity. All attachment implies fear, for all things are transient. And fear makes one a slave. This freedom from attachment does not come with practice; it is natural, when one knows one's true being. Self-knowledge is detachment. All craving is due to a sense of insufficiency. When you know that you lack nothing, that all there is, is you and yours, desire ceases.

There is the body and there is the Self. Between them is the mind, in which the Self is reflected as "I am". Because of the imperfections of the mind, its crudity and restlessness, lack of discernment and insight, it takes itself to be the body, not the Self. All that is needed is to purify the mind so that it can realize its identity with the Self. When the mind merges in the Self, the body presents no problems. It remains what it is, an instrument of cognition and action, the tool and the expression of the creative fire within. The ultimate value of the body is that it serves to discover the cosmic body, which is the universe in its entirety. As you realize yourself in manifestation, you keep on discovering that you are ever more than what you have imagined.

There is the body. Inside the body appears to be an observer, and outside a world under observation. The observer and his observation as well as the world observed appear and disappear together. Beyond it all, there is void. This void is one for all.

Freedom is from something. What are you to be free from? Obviously, you must be free from the person you take yourself to be, for it is the idea you have of yourself that keeps you in bondage.

There is the true Awareness, from which comes consciousness, which is your feeling 'I am', be one with your consciousness and that is all that you can do, the Ultimate must come to you. You can only watch what happens – there is nothing you can do to get it.

From deep sleep to the waking state, what is it? It is the 'I am' state with no words, later the words start flowing and you get involved with the meaning of the words and carry out your worldly life with the meaning of those words – that is the mind. But before the 'I am' and waking state, that borderline, there you have to be.

There is no reason why this consciousness came about, but once it comes about, it cannot stand still, consciousness is the same as movement. That movement takes place through the three gunas, which are inherent in this knowledge 'I am'. All movement takes place through these gunas and this consciousness keeps on humming.

From deep sleep you wake up, that border is Paravani, beyond words. When you move, become conscious, you feel 'I am', then mind takes charge, words take over and you are embroiled in the world. Paravani is other than language, 'Para' means 'other' or 'transcend' – the language of just being without words.

From the no-knowing state, the first veil I took was that of 'I am', that was formless, nameless. But I embraced the body: I got a form for myself; I got a name for myself. This was the fall. Therefore all sages advise: Give up the shackles of the body! 'I am the body' – these are the shackles. Give them up.

There is no second, or higher self to search for. You are the highest self, only give up the false ideas you have about yourself.

There is no separate God to propitiate and get things done according to our will. Without doing anything you have the knowledge 'I am'. Immense courage, heroism and conviction that

There is no such thing as peace of mind. Mind means disturbance; restlessness itself is mind.

Get rid of all ideas about yourself, even of the idea that you are God. No self-definition is valid.

Get stabilized in the primary concept 'I am' in order to lose it and be free from all concepts. In understanding the unreality of 'I am' you are totally free from it.

There is nothing for you to do, everything just comes into being and happens. Why are you concerned with what to do? You deal with the world only after having Consciousness, when the 'I am' is there. Once it is gone everything ends, it is all spontaneous.

Get to know that 'I am' without words, which arises in the morning. Knowing the Self, abiding in the Self-knowledge, is not a mere intellectual knowing. You must be that, and you should not move away from it. Remain firm.

There is no effort in witnessing. You understand that you are the witness only, and the understanding acts. You need nothing more, just remember that you are the witness only.

Give up all and you gain all. Then life becomes what it was meant to be: pure radiation from an inexhaustible source. In that light the world appears dimly like a dream.

Give up all questions except one 'who am I?' After all the only fact you are sure of is that you 'are'. The 'I am' is certain, the 'I am this' is not. Struggle to find out what you are in reality.

There is no difference in the types of 'I amness', I experience fatigue now, good health earlier, but the common factor is beingness which has not changed. All is illusion, the 'I am' is knowledge, but it's also an illusion, say what you like, nothing prevails, except the knowledge 'you are'. You presume that the world has existed without your beingness; your world is with your arrival, not prior to it, if you are not, your world is not.

There is no explanation for how this seed, this consciousness or knowledge 'I am' has arisen. But once it is in existence, it cannot stand still – that is, consciousness is tantamount to 'movement'. And all movement takes place through the 'gunas', which are inherent in the knowledge 'I am'. This consciousness keeps on 'humming' – (Maharaj uses the Marathi word 'gun-gun', which means the humming sound or the humming of the 'gunas') – and expresses itself through the three 'gunas'.

Give your heart and mind to brooding over the 'I am', what is it, how is it, what is its source, its life, its meaning. It is very much like digging a well. You reject all that is not water, till you reach the life-giving spring.

Go deep into the sense of 'I am' and you will find. How do you find a thing you have mislaid or forgotten? You keep it in your mind until you recall it. The sense of being, of 'I am' is the first to emerge. Ask yourself whence it comes or just watch it quietly. When the mind stays in the 'I am', without moving, you enter a state, which cannot be verbalized, but which can be experienced. All you need to do is to try and try again. After all the sense of 'I am' is always with you, only you have attached all kinds of things to it- body, feelings, thoughts, ideas, possessions and so on. All these self-identifications are misleading, because of these you take yourself to be what you are not.

There is no need of a way out [of the dream]! Don't you see that a way out is also a part of the dream? All you have to do is see the dream as dream. The very idea of going beyond the dream is illusory. Why go anywhere? Just realize that you are dreaming a dream you call the world, and stop looking for ways out. The problem is not the dream. Your problem is that you like one part of your dream and not another. Love all, or none of it, and stop complaining. When you have seen the dream as a dream, you have done all that needs be done.

Go on to know the 'I am' without words, you must be that and not deviate from it for even a moment, and then it will disappear.

Go to the 'I am' state, remain there, merge, and go beyond. If you were to dwell in the 'I am' and firmly abide in it, all external things will lose their grip on you.

There is no proprietor behind that feeling of awareness. It only is, it is beyond description, and words cannot be of any use. That is the permanent state and this manifestation is only its movement. Nobody becomes a 'Parabrahman', nobody 'can' become a 'Parabrahman': It is. Before the knowledge 'I am' appeared on you, that is 'Parabrahman'. If you revert properly, the consciousness 'I am', will disappear, then there is no movement. Go to the root and you conclude 'I am'… yes… yes…, you say 'I am', without words. Investigation will reveal that it is a result of the five elemental play. There is another principle that observes the 'I am' and the elemental play.

Go to the source and be established there, then, there is no change. You might have read the Gita, who is there to judge its soundness? The knowledge 'I am' has to approve whatever is said there. Establish yourself in the Self, whatever you are prior to the 'I am', get established there. When this abidance in the Self is achieved, all talks with sound gibberish.

There are no individuals; there are only food bodies with the knowledge 'I am'. There is no difference between and ant, human being and 'Iswara' they are of the same quality. The body of an ant is small; an elephant's is large. The strength is different, because of size, but the life-force is the same. For knowledge the body is necessary.

There are various types of charity, but the greatest charity is the renunciation of the knowledge 'I am'. When you give that up you escape birth and death. Waking state represents activity; deep sleep represents peace, quiet. When these two are present it means 'I am' is there, but you the Absolute are neither the waking state, deep sleep nor the 'I amness'.

Guru means the 'I amness' itself, which always reminds you 'I am', 'I am', 'I am' – that is guru-guru-guru, like the sound of a motorcar starting. It is a continuous reminder that you are.

Having acquired and understood the knowledge 'I am' stay there in seclusion and don't wander around here and there. Once you stabilize in the 'I am', you will realize that it is not the eternal state, but 'you' are eternal and ancient.

There being no vital breath, the knowledge of 'I amness' is absent. Take full advantage of the naturally available capital with you – that is, your life force and the knowledge 'I am'; they always go hand in hand. Right now, exploit it to the utmost. All worldly activities are going on only because of the knowledge 'I am' together with that motive force which is the life force, the vital breath. And that is not something apart from you; you are that only. Investigate and study this exclusively, abide in that, worship that only.

Having perfected the mirror so that it reflects correctly, truly, you can turn the mirror round and see in it a reflection of yourself -true as far as the mirror can reflect. But the reflection is not yourself - you are the seer of the reflection. Do understand it clearly - whatever you may perceive, you are not what you perceive. You can see both the image and the mirror. You are neither.

There can be no experience beyond consciousness. Yet there is the experience of just being. There is a state beyond consciousness, which is not unconscious. Some call it super-consciousness, or pure consciousness, or supreme consciousness. It is pure awareness free from the subject-object nexus. Consciousness is intermittent, full of gaps. Yet there is the continuity of identity. What is this sense of identity due to, if not to something beyond consciousness?

There is no 'I' apart from the body or the world. The three appear and disappear together. At the root is the sense 'I am'. Go beyond it. The idea 'I-am-not-body' is merely an antidote to the idea 'I-am-the-body', which is false. What is that 'I am'? Unless you know yourself, what else can you know?

Having collected all the knowledge, ponder over it in seclusion.

The world has only as much power over you as you give it. Rebel. Go beyond duality.

The world is but a show, glittering and empty. It is, and yet it is not. It is there as long as I want to see it and take part in it. When I cease caring, it dissolves. It has no cause and serves no purpose. It just happens when we are absent-minded. It appears exactly as it looks, but there is no depth in it, nor meaning. Only the onlooker is real, call him Self or Atma. To the Self, the world is but a colorful show, which he enjoys as long as it lasts and forgets when it is over. Whatever happens on the stage makes him shudder in terror or roll with laughter, yet all the time he is aware that it is but a show. Without desire or fear, he enjoys it, as it happens.

Having realized that you cannot influence the results, pay no attention to your desire and fears. Let them come and go. Don't give them the nourishment of interest and attention.

The world of 'Maya' is built up of concepts only. I cannot charge the world with giving me the pain; the whole cause of the pain is the knowingness 'I am'. When this knowledge was not there was there any pain or pleasure?

Having seen that you are a bundle of memories held together by attachment, step out and look from the outside. You may perceive for the first time something which is not memory. You cease to be Mr.-so-and-so, busy about his own affairs. You are at last at peace. You realize that nothing was ever wrong with the world, you alone were wrong and now it is all over. Never again will you be caught in the meshes of desire born of ignorance.

Theoretically you always have a chance for self-realization. In practice a situation must arise, when all the factors necessary for self-realization are present. This need not discourage you. Your dwelling on the fact of 'I am' will soon create another chance. For attitude attracts opportunity. All you know is second-hand. Only 'I am' is first-hand and needs no proofs. Stay with it.

He who is beyond time – is the un-nameable. A glowing ember moved round and round quickly enough appears as a glowing circle. When the movement ceases, the ember remains. Similarly, the 'I am' in movement creates the world. The 'I am' at peace becomes the Absolute.

Here is an article before it came into existence, what was its name? From non-being into the being state, how was it observed? You just felt that touch. Before observing anything we feel the touch of 'I am'. To realize that state prior to conception, that eternal state, whatever that state is, to abide in that is the highest. Now, for your sake, I attach a name to it, the 'Parabrahman' state – the Absolute.

Hold on to the 'I am' very firmly, ever abide in it and it'll dissolve, then you are as you are.

Hold on to the sense 'I am' to the exclusion of everything else. When this mind becomes completely silent, it shines with a new light and vibrates with new knowledge. It all comes spontaneously; you need only to hold on to the 'I am'.

The witness is not indifferent. He is the fullness of understanding and compassion. Only as the witness you can help another.

The witnessing of the 'Ishwara' state occurs to Me. 'Ishwara' is the manifestation of the five elements and the universe. The witnessing of the 'I amness' occurs to the Absolute. A disciple (Sadhaka) who is getting established in the 'Ishwara' principle should not claim this understanding (Siddha).

The words of 'prana' signify mind. So how could there be mind without vital force? This vital force and the consciousness (that is, the knowledge 'I am' or the beingness and the mind) appear simultaneously and always exist together.

The world appears to you so overwhelmingly real because you think of it all the time; cease thinking of it and it will dissolve into thin mist.

The world does not yield to changing. By its very nature it is painful and transient. See it as it is and divest yourself of all desire and fear. When the world does not hold and bind you, it becomes an abode of joy and beauty. You can be happy in the world only when you are free of it.

The vital force carries out all the activities. The mind communicates, and the knowledge 'I am' is merely a witness; this is the actual state of affairs. But all these – that is, food body quintessence, and the knowledge 'I am', the vital breath and the mind – these are all a temporary phase only; so long as the food essence is available, the knowingness will last.

The whole life is endured and sustained by the knowledge particle, 'I am'. Without 'I am' there is no life. They are interdependent, not one without the other. I am prior to the 'I am', which is true, eternal and immutable. Beingness, world and body are time bound, your life is not forever, it rises and sets like the waking and sleeping states alternate. The totality of manifestation thrives as long as the beingness is there.

How amusing it is to see someone who thinks of himself as an individual, who thinks of himself as a doer or achiever. Whatever is happening and the experiencing of the happening, takes place in this consciousness when the 'I am' arises.

The whole universe is experienced in the consciousness 'I am'. If that is not there, what else can ever exist? This consciousness is beating a drum; everyone is carried away by the noise of the drum. Who looks for the drummer? Who is sounding and beating the drum? It is so amazing that no one casts even a glance at this speck of consciousness.

The window is the absence of the wall, and it gives air and light because it is empty. Be empty of all mental content, of all imagination and effort, and the very absence of obstacles will cause reality to rush in.

The witness and consciousness appear and disappear together. The witness or the sense 'I am' too is transient but is given importance to break the spell of the known; the illusion that only the perceivable is real. Presently for you perception is primary and witnessing secondary, revert it to make witnessing primary and perception secondary (The 'I am' is just a device to revert).

The vital breath gets conditioned or manacled by the bondage of name. It accepts the name as 'I am'; this is the mistake. That which is deconditioned from name and form is 'Paramatman'. That which is conditioned by the body, mind, name and form is called 'jiva'. The language of the vital breath is mind, and the mind is the motive force for all activities.

How can you retain the pride that I am like this? This 'I am' business depends entirely on the food essence. So how can you retain it perpetually – that I shall remain like this only? To extract any essence, water is very necessary, and the water quality is bound to dry up.

How can you speak or develop any concept unless the primary concept 'I am' is available? This primary concept begets further concepts, that is, all other concepts occur to it. However, whatever concept occurs to you, including the primary concept 'I am', is not the eternal state.

The teacher tells the watcher you are not this; there is nothing yours in this, except the point of 'I am', which is the bridge between the watcher and his dream. 'I am this', 'I am that' is a dream, while pure 'I am' has the stamp of reality on it. You have tasted so many things – all came to naught. Only the sense 'I am' persisted – unchanged. Stay with the changeless among the changeful, until you are able to go beyond.

How did I get this birth? That is the point on which I persist in finding the answer; I 'must' know this. When I was told 'sattva', then what is 'sattva'? 'Sattva' is the essence of the five elements. In that essence, in that juice, lies the knowledge 'I am'; but all that is still of the five elements. Then how did this come about? My guru told me the whole story. Thus I came to know it is ignorance, and I know from experience, that everybody is starting from there. Thus whatever has come about is sheer ignorance, and we are nothing more, that is what my guru told me.

The teaching is simple, when the 'I am' arises, everything appears, when 'I am' subsides everything disappears. Onto your Absoluteness, which is without form or shape, came this knowledge 'I am', which is also without shape and form.

The thing which attracts you most of all is your 'I amness'. You want to retain that 'I amness'. You want to 'Be'. This 'I am' is what you truly love most. You want to be alive.

The Ultimate you can never be lost; whatever you have lost, you have lost only words. The Ultimate you knows or feels 'I am' without words. Through this 'I am' comes the world knowledge. You are not in isolation; you are part and parcel of the world knowledge.

How do you know that you do not know yourself? Your direct insight tells you that your self you know first, for nothing exists without your being there to experience its existence. You imagine you do not know yourself, because you cannot describe yourself. You can only say: "I know that I am" and you will refuse as untrue the statement "I am not". But whatever can be described cannot be yourself, and what you are cannot be described. You can only know your being by being yourself without any attempt at self-definition and self-description. Once you have understood that you are nothing perceivable or conceivable, that whatever appears in the field of consciousness cannot be yourself, you will apply yourself to the eradication of all self-identification, as the only way that can take you to a deeper realization of yourself.

The very core of this consciousness is the quality 'I am', there is no personality or individual there, reside there and transcend it.

How does one recognize this 'atman'? It is by understanding the knowledge 'I am' – the 'atma-jnana'. Just as space is all-pervading, so the knowledge 'I am' is all-pervading, limitless and infinite. How strange, such a supreme principle is treated as though it is a body! All the sufferings are due to this mistaken identity. If you give the highest honor due to it, you will not undergo either suffering or death.

The body-mind is like a room. It is there, but I need not live in it all the time.

How does personality come into being? By identifying the present with the past and projecting it into the future.

The sense of 'I am' is your own. You cannot part with it, but you can impart it to anything, as in saying, I am young; I am rich, and so on. But such self-identifications are patently false and the cause of bondage.

How was I in the absence of the message 'I am' – that is, prior to beingness? I provided you with the name tags for that state. These titles are 'Parabrahman', 'Paramatman' etc.; they are only pointers to the state, but not the state itself. In the Ultimate they are redundant, extraneous and bogus.

The sense of taste comes from the element earth, perception emanates from air and sound from space, but the primary concept is 'I am'. First without sound you know 'I am' (as when you awaken from deep sleep), then you say 'I am', with this comes the need 'to be'. With the departure of the vital breath, there is no sound, no language, no warmth – its death, death is also a concept. Nevertheless, everything dwells in food essence quality ('I am'), when this disappears – it is all over. To sustain beingness, the product of food, we eat food, but that is not your identity.

The sense that 'you are' is a big thing. What is most significant is the fact that you remember your sense of being, subsequently all other things appear. Earlier this memory 'I am' was not and suddenly it appeared. Now I expound on the spiritual talk called 'niroopana'. In Marathi the word 'niroopana' is derived from the word 'niroopa' (nirope), which means 'message'. Therefore, to deliver any spiritual talk that is 'niroopana', the primary message 'I am' must first be present, then whatever ensues from this primary message will be the spiritual talk.

The subtle body is created with the emergence of the 'I am' idea. The two are one. It is momentary. Real when present, unreal when over. Call it empirical, or actual, or factual. It is the reality of immediate experience, here and now, which cannot be denied. You can question the description and the meaning, but not the event itself. Being and non-being alternate and their reality is momentary. The immutable reality lies beyond space and time. Realize the momentariness of being and non-being and be free from both.

The talk about myself is the talk about yourself. Let any worthy one reach to any heights, anywhere, but it is time-bound. Any height! It is just a passage of time. Time means the Sun – the world is because of it – beingness. The sum total means 'you are', beingness only, when the knowledge 'I am' sets, the world is liquidated, Nivritti – no message 'I am'.

The tangle which is entirely below the level of consciousness can be set right by being with yourself, the 'I am', by watching yourself in your daily life with alert interest with the intention to understand rather than to judge, in full acceptance of whatever may emerge, because it is there, you encourage the deep to come to the surface and enrich your life and consciousness with its captive energies. This is the great work of awareness; it removes obstacles and releases energies by understanding the nature of life and mind. Intelligence is the door to freedom and alert attention is the mother of intelligence.

I am dead already. Physical death will make no difference in my case. I am timeless being. I am free of desire or fear, because I do not remember the past, or imagine the future. Where there are no names and shapes, how can there be desires and fear? With desirelessness comes timelessness. I am safe, because what is not cannot touch what is. You feel unsafe, because you imagine danger. Of course, your body as such is complex and vulnerable and needs protection. But not you. Once you realize your own unassailable being, you will be at peace.

I am experiencing the manifest world but prior to it I experience the 'Bindu', the point. When I am that Bindu, everything is, the world also is. The Bindu and the world are not two. 'Bin' means without and 'du' means two, so, no duality. Bindu – the point of 'I amness', I experience that. What is it? It is the very experience of the five elements and the three gunas – the whole universe. That is my intimate relationship with that 'I am' only – Bindu only.

I am now 74 years old. And yet I feel that I am an infant. I feel clearly that in spite of all the changes I am a child. My Guru told me that the child, which is you even now, is your real self ('swarupa'). Go back to that state of pure being, where the 'I am' is still in its purity before it gets contaminated with 'this I am' or 'that I am'. Your burden is of false self-identification – abandon them all. My Guru told me – 'Trust me. I tell you, you are divine. Take it as the absolute truth. Your joy is divine; your suffering is divine too. All comes from God. Remember it always. You are God, your will alone is done.' I did believe him and soon realized how wonderfully true and accurate were his words. I did not condition my mind by thinking: 'I am God, I am wonderful, I am beyond.' I simply followed his instruction, which was to focus the mind on pure being, 'I am' and stay in it. I used to sit for hours together, with nothing but the 'I am' in my mind and soon peace and joy and a deep all-embracing love became my normal state. In it all disappeared - myself, my Guru, the life I lived, the world around me. Only peace remained and unfathomable silence.

The seeker is he who is in search of himself. Soon he discovers that his own body he cannot be. Once the conviction "I am not the body" becomes so well grounded that he can no longer feel, think and act for and behalf of the body, he will easily discover that he is the universal being, knowing, acting; that in him and through him the entire universe is real, conscious and alive. This is the heart of the problem. Either you are body-conscious and a slave of circumstances, or you are the universal consciousness itself - and in full control of every event. Yet consciousness, individual or universal, is not my true abode; I am not in it, it is not mine, there is no "me" in it. I am beyond, though it is not easy to explain how one can be neither conscious nor unconscious, but just beyond. I cannot say that I am in God or I am God; God is the universal light and love, the universal witness: I am beyond the universal even.

The self is universal and its aims are universal. There is nothing personal about the self.

I am talking about knowledge, whatever knowledge the 'I am' is, it's the knowledge. You are living to sustain that knowledge 'I am', hence you struggle. If that knowledge is gone, what interest could you have? You are like a doctor taking care, the knowledge 'you are' is nourishing and protecting the body. Remember this, if you want to remember me, remember the knowledge 'I am'. Ancestors told us to meditate on me, remember me, but they also said that the knowledge 'I am' is me too.

The sense 'I am' is composed of pure light and the sense of being. The 'I' is there even without the 'am'. So is the pure light there, whether you say 'I' or not. Become aware of that pure light and you will never lose it. The beingness in being, the awareness in consciousness, the interest in every experience – that is not describable, yet perfectly accessible, for there is nothing else.

The sense of 'I am' is always there; only when it identifies with the body it is called the ego.

The sense of 'I am' is both unreal and real. Unreal when I say 'I am this or that'. It is real when we mean 'I am not this nor that'. The 'I am' and the witness are not one, but without one the other cannot be.

The self you want to know, is it some second self? Are you made of several selves? Surely, there is only one self and you are that self. The self you are is the only self there is. Remove and abandon your wrong ideas about yourself and there it is, in all its glory.

I am trying to speak of my most intimate secrets. Just as the dream world, uncalled for, has appeared and you observe it, similarly this world, uncalled for, has appeared and you are compelled to observe it. Just observe. Spontaneously, unknowingly, your beingness has appeared. Knowingly you don't know 'Now I am going to be'; only after the formation of 'I amness' do you know 'I am'.

I call a 'siddha' one who has attained the ultimate, in that ultimate state, the devotee and God, the 'maya' (primary illusion) and the 'Brahman' have disappeared. And, there is no beneficiary or experiencer of all that, because he is without the concept 'I am'. He does not know 'I am', he does not know that he exists in that state, that knowingness is completely obliterated.

I don't discuss Brahman or Maya; I tell you my story which is your story as well. With Atmajnana (Self-knowledge) the 'I' consciousness is not there. Then I don't worry about God or illusion. The 'I am' is the starting point of both misery and happiness.

The problem is not yours - it is your mind's only. Begin by disassociating yourself from your mind. Resolutely remind yourself that you are not the mind and that its problems are not yours.

I find that somehow, by shifting the focus of attention, I become the very thing I look at, and experience the kind of consciousness it has; I become the inner witness of the thing. I call this capacity of entering other focal points of consciousness, love; you may give it any name you like. Love says "I am everything". Wisdom says "I am nothing". Between the two, my life flows. Since at any point of time and space I can be both the subject and the object of experience, I express it by saying that I am both, and neither, and beyond both.

The question of resistance [to reincarnation] does not arise. What is born and reborn is not you. Let it happen, watch it happen.

The riddle of spirituality cannot be solved by the intellect. At the most, your intellect can provide you with livelihood. Whatever you try to become, that is not you. Before the words come out, before you say 'I am', that is you. You must be concerned with only yourself. Don't worry about anybody else. What are you?

The scriptures say that we have our 'karma' and our sin and that is why we are here, but this is for the ignorant masses. One who has realized the self-knowledge 'I am' for him these stories are of no use.

I have been very open, very explicit. I've been telling you that you are not the body, you are that knowledge only and that vital breath is your conveyance, a tool by which you carry out your activities, and the knowledge 'I am' is very subtle. Because of your knowledge, you are and world is.

I have experienced all four kinds of speech and transcended them. Rarely will anybody follow this hierarchy to stabilize in the consciousness and transcend consciousness. Starting from 'Vaikhari' (word), normally we listen to words; from 'Vaikhari' we go to 'Madhyama' (mind-thought); in watching the mind we are in 'Pashayanti' where the concept formation takes place and from there to 'Para' ('I am' without words), and finally from 'Para' to prior to consciousness. This is the line to follow, but only a rare one follows it – receding, reversing.

I have many photographs of my Guru here, because my Guru 'is' I know 'I am'. You presume that your Guru is a body-mind and that is a mistake. I do not look upon my Guru like that. He is merged into Consciousness and I see him as that.

I know that this manifest Brahman or Cosmos is unreal, timebound and unstable. The message 'I am' has spontaneously come and is the root of the manifested world. The message 'I am', caught hold of the body as its identity and suffering started. The 'I am' happened and the world was cooked up. Even this information, you got later, when the 'I am' came into friction, recognized the body, mother and so on, prior to that you did not have the message 'I am', you existed, but you did not know.

The primary concept is the 'I am', out of it are created all other concepts. You have come from the primary concept, so long as you have the need to be, you have this prolific wonderful world and all the Gods are available. The distinction between the world and Brahman has come because you want to sustain your beingness, the 'I am', the manifest world is made important by you because you want to be. Whatever without it (consciousness) is perfect. Only that is, nothing else. My body is universal, not individualistic. What is this 'I am' business? Understand it and be apart from it, transcend it. Just be.

The primary illusion is only this knowingness 'I am', prior to that there was no illusion. This very consciousness is the source of illusion. This illusion or consciousness or 'I amness' does not remain as something eternal. It is liberated; this non-eternal consciousness is liberated, when the knowingness is transformed into non-knowingness; that is liberation.

The primary miracle is that I experience 'I am' and the world. Prior to this experiencing, I abided in myself, in my eternal Absolute state. Without my beingness – that is, without the message 'I am' – my eternal Absolute state only prevails.

The primary occurrence is the reminder 'I am' and out of which springs the language and the talk. So, what is this 'I amness'? Remember that it is in the primary reminder 'I am' that the whole cosmos and your body exist. Who and from where is this sense of being? This has to be thoroughly investigated. When this is done, while abiding necessarily in the knowledge 'I am' – the sense of beingness – an amazing revelation will be made, namely that from your own seed-beingness the whole manifest universe is projected including your body. This supreme and powerful principle, though being itself without form and name, upon sensing 'I am' instantly embraces the body and mistakenly accepts this as its own. It clings to the body-identity so quickly that the fact of its own independent existence is easily missed.

The problem arises only when the memory of past pains and pleasures, which are essential to all organic life, remains as a reflex, dominating behavior. This reflex takes the shape of "I" and uses the body and the mind for its purposes, which are invariably in search for pleasure or flight from pain. When you recognize the "I" as it is, a bundle of desires and fears, and the sense of "mine" as embracing all things and people needed for the purpose of avoiding pain and securing pleasure, you will see that the "I" and the "mine" are false ideas, having no foundation in reality. Created by the mind, they rule their creator as long as it takes them to be true; when questioned, they dissolve. The "I" and "mine", having no existence in themselves, need a support which they find in the body. The body becomes their point of reference. When you talk of "my" husband and "my children", you mean the body's husband and the body's children. Give up the idea of being the body and face the question: Who am I? At once a process will be set in motion which will bring back reality, or rather, will take mind to reality.

I never seek anything from anybody else. Whatever I want to get, I get it out of my own being, I worship that very principle 'I am' and demand what I want out of that; because of that all these things are coming.

I repeatedly tell you that there is nothing save this consciousness, the knowledge 'I am' – if you feel like worshipping something, worship that, I am giving blessings. Blessings mean what? I am giving confidence and courage.

I want to take you to that 'I am' concept which is the last outpost of illusion and get rid of it. Understand the quality of these concepts.

I was always listening to that sacred recitation (Japa, also known as Ajapajapa - 'So hum') which was constantly happening inside me. The primary cause of this Japa is the knowledge that you have of 'I am'

The one, who tries to abide in the Self, loses identity with his ego. The very identity that 'I am' gets dissolved. Your true identity – The Absolute – is prior to the 'I am'. How can you provide a uniform (the ochre robe) to it?

The only spiritual way to understanding you true nature is to find out the source of this concept 'I am'. Before the sense of presence arrived I was in that state in which the concept of time was never there. So what is born? It is the concept of time, and that event which is birth, living, and death together constitute nothing but time, duration.

I was taught to give attention to my sense of 'I am' and I found it supremely effective. Therefore, I can speak of it with full confidence. But often people come with bodies, brains and minds so mishandled, perverted and weak that the state of formless attention is beyond them. In such cases some simpler token of earnestness (like repeating a 'mantra') is appropriate. After all it is the earnestness that is indispensable, the crucial factor. 'Sadhana' is only a vessel and it must be filled to be brim with earnestness, which is but love in action. For nothing can be done without love.

The people who begin their sadhana are so feverish and restless that they have to be very busy to keep themselves on the track. An absorbing routine is good for them. After some time, they quieten down and turn away from effort. In peace and silence, the skin of the "I" dissolves and the inner and the outer become one. The real sadhana is effortless.

The person is merely the result of a misunderstanding. In reality, there is no such thing. Feelings, thoughts and actions race before the watcher in endless succession, leaving traces in the brain and creating an illusion of continuity. A reflection of the watcher in the mind creates the sense of "I" and the person acquires an apparently independent existence. In reality there is no person, only the watcher identifying himself with the "I" and the "mine".

If petty worldly knowledge has no form, then can the knowledge 'I am' or Ishwara state have any form? If you accept this, then accept it and go and don't go elsewhere, just dwell there. Let any activity happen through your knowledge 'I am', which has no form, but is its witness only. The knowledge 'you are' has no form, so also for other knowledge. 'You are' is the primary knowledge.

The person merges into the witness, the witness into awareness, awareness into pure being, yet identity is not lost, only its limitations are lost. It is transfigured and becomes the real Self, the sadguru, the eternal friend and guide. You cannot approach it in worship. No external activity can reach the inner self; worship and prayers remain on the surface only; to do deeper meditation is essential, the striving to go beyond the states of sleep, dream and waking. In the beginning the attempts are irregular, then they recur more often, become regular, then continuous and intense, until all obstacles are conquered.

If this is ignorance, then where is my beingness? My beingness is in a town which is no-town, in a place which is no-place. How did this come about? Because of the knowledge 'I am', which is ignorance. Maya, which came about suddenly, without my asking. Once having come about, this Maya liked what it had created and it wanted that beingness to last for all time. Maya embraced it with such fierceness, that, at any cost, it wants to prolong the existence of that beingness as long as it can.

If you are able to establish yourself in the vital breath as you are, you become manifest. The vital breath, when it is conditioned by the body, you call it personality. But as matter the vital breath is spread all over, it is manifest; it is universal. If you establish in the vital breath as 'I am', that in itself will get you there. Don't be dishonest to your vital breath, worship it, and when you do so, it can lead you anywhere, to any heights – this is the quintessence of my talks. In such simplified fashion, nobody has expounded this profound teaching.

The mirror can do nothing to attract the sun. It can only keep bright. As soon as the mind is ready, the sun shines in. [The light] is uncaused and unvarying by itself, and colored by the mind as soon as it moves and changes. It is very much like a cinema. The light is not in the film, but the film colors the light and makes it appear to move by intercepting it.

The moment the 'I amness' explodes or appears, all of space is lit up. The entire sky is the expression of your Beingness, yet you believe that you are only the body. Your love for the body limits your horizons. But the moment those walls come down, you are one with 'Brahman' and the whole universe.

If you are angry or in pain, separate yourself from anger and pain and watch them. Externalization is the first step to liberation. Step away and look. The physical events will go on happening, but by themselves they have no importance. It is the mind alone that matters. If you could only keep quiet, clear of memories and expectations, you would be able to discern the beautiful pattern of events. It is your restlessness that causes chaos.

The next elevation will only come when you abide in the Self.

If you do not have the knowledge 'I am' who is going to seek? You must be, only then the search can begin. Remember the knowledge 'I am' – that alone pervades everything – be only that and give up the rest.

The one who abides in that principle by which he knows 'I am' knows all and does not require anything.

The one who abides in that principle by which he knows 'I am', he is the manifest. He abides in that manifest 'Brahman' all the twenty-four hours. Whether the body remains or not, that manifest self-principle always remains. You must continually remember, 'chew the cud', that the knowledge 'I am' signifies knowing all gods, all the 'Vedas', it is the 'Brahman' only. You must continually think about it, and should in the course of such reminiscing, the body drop off, then, that consciousness will definitely be the highest.

The one witness reflects itself in the countless bodies as 'I am'. As long as the bodies, however subtle, last, the 'I am' appears as many. Beyond the body there is only the One.

If you have questions, ask the one who wants to know. Cling to the questioner – that is your own Beingness, or 'I amness'. Once you have done that people will approach you, they will call you a Mahatma or Anandmayi.

If you have regard for me remember my words. The knowledge 'I am' is the greatest God, the Guru, be one with that, be intimate with it. That itself will bless you with all the knowledge relevant for you in the proliferation of that knowledge, it will lead you to the state which is eternal. The message 'I am' has no form, it is only a food container. It is there, it has meaning, you cannot perceive it, observe it. The message 'I am' is time-bound. The principle to which 'I am' refers is beyond time, timeless, eternal.

The message 'I am' is there. The mind flow is also there; it is not a personality, it is the consciousness. The very idea that you are the body is ridiculous; the consciousness is experiencing its manifestation. A rare being will realize this.

If you identify yourself as the body, such an identity must be let go off, sacrificed. Your real identity has no body and no thought. And that self, the spontaneous knowledge 'I am' is what you are. Since the self is not the body, the self is neither male nor female. You must fulfill the vow that you are not the body but solely the indwelling principle 'I am'.

If you sit here quietly, being one with the knowledge 'I am', then you are not concerned with the world or what goes on in the world. It is only when the consciousness starts operating and there are various movements in the consciousness that the behavior in the world takes place. When I am not conscious of the existence of the body, experiences are not registered.

If you stand aloof as observer only, you will not suffer. You will see the world as a show, a most entertaining show indeed.

The mind is discontinuous. Again and again it blanks out, like in sleep or swoon or distraction. There must be something continuous to register discontinuity. Memory is always partial, unreliable and evanescent. It does not explain the strong sense of identity pervading consciousness, the sense "I am". Find out what is at the root of it.

The mind produces thoughts ceaselessly, even when you do not look at them. When you know what is going on in your mind, you call it consciousness. This is your waking state - your consciousness shifts from sensation to sensation, from perception to perception, from idea to idea, in endless succession. Then comes awareness, the direct insight into the whole of consciousness, the totality of the mind. The mind is like a river, flowing ceaselessly in the bed of the body; you identify yourself for a moment with some particular ripple and call it "my thought". All you are conscious of is your mind; awareness is the cognizance of consciousness as a whole.

If you stay with the idea that you are not the body nor the mind, not even their witness, but altogether beyond, your mind will grow in clarity, your desires in purity, your actions in charity, and that inner distillation will take you to another world, a world of truth and fearless love. Resist your old habits of feeling and thinking; keep on telling yourself: "No, not so, it cannot be so; I am not like this, I do not need it, I do not want it", and a day will surely come when the entire structure of error and despair will collapse and the ground will be free for a new life.

If you want to remember this visit, if you have love for me, remember this 'I am' principle and without the command or direction of this principle, do nothing.

Immortality is freedom from the feeling 'I am', to have that freedom remain in the sense 'I am'. The knowledge that is prior to thought – 'I am' – is covered by a human body which food with the vital breath and knowledge of the Self (Prana and Jnana). This means that you are only covered by a human body. Once you reach that state of 'I am' through your attention you will only be aware of 'That' and you will no longer be affected by all of these tendencies (Vasanas). You will have transcended them.

In deep meditation, infused only with the knowledge 'I am', it will be intuitively revealed to you as to how this 'I amness' came to be.

In deep sleep you are not a self-conscious person, yet you are alive. When you are alive and conscious, but no longer self-conscious, you are not a person any more. During the waking hours you are, as if on the stage, playing a role, but what are you when the play is over? You are what you are; what you were before the play began you remain when it is over. Look at yourself as performing on the stage of life. The performance may be splendid or clumsy, but you are not in it, you merely watch it; with interest and sympathy, of course, but keeping in mind all the time that you are only watching while the play -life- is going on.

In deep sleep, consciousness was in a dormant condition, there were no bodies, no concepts, and no encumbrances. Upon the arrival of this apparently wakeful state, with the arrival of the concept 'I am', the love of 'I am' woke up. That itself is 'Maya', illusion.

The letters 'I am' are written spontaneously with a certain ink. What is that ink which was used to write that which you are? In that ink with which the letters 'I am' were written, in that ink of the title of 'Tej Sesh Bhagavan' is confirmed by the 'Vedas'. 'Sesh' means the leftover, the remains. That 'Tej Sesh Bhagavan' has come spontaneously and will spontaneously go. The firm conviction that I am this, the three states – waking state, deep sleep and the knowledge 'I am' – are the aspects of that 'Tej Sesh Bhagavan'. You are not that.

The manifestation of the dynamic immanent Spirit is in the form of the guna (quality) 'I am'; it understands itself as 'I am'. Then this guna involves itself in the activities in the world through the three gunas. That is the quality.

In dream you love some and not others. On waking up you find you are love itself, embracing all. Personal love, however intense and genuine, invariably binds; love in freedom is love of all. When you are love itself, you are beyond time and numbers. In loving one you love all, in loving all, you love each.

The memory of the past unfulfilled desires traps energy, which manifests itself as a person. When its charge gets exhausted, the person dies. Unfulfilled desires are carried over into the next birth. I do not say that the same person is reborn. It dies and dies for good. But its memories remain and their desires and fears. They supply the energy for a new person. The real takes no part in it, but makes it possible by giving it the light.

The message 'I am' does not have any form, design, or color. So long as 'I am' is, this experience of manifestation is, once that 'I amness' disappears there is no experience. Once this message 'I am' appears in insect, animal, or human being, immediately the manifestation occurs with that beingness. Inside and outside is full of manifestation. These talks are not for general consumption, or the masses.

In my original true state I have no form and no thoughts. I didn't know I was, but suddenly another state appeared in which I had a form and thought, 'I am'. How did this appear? The one who explains how these appearances have come about is the Sat-Guru.

In peace and silence, the skin of the "I" dissolves and the inner and the outer become one.

In reality you were never born and never shall die. But now you imagine that you are, or have, a body and you ask what has brought about this state. Within the limits of illusion the answer is: desire born from memory attracts you to a body and makes you think as one with it. But this is true only from the relative point of view. In fact, there is no body, nor a world to contain it; there is only a mental condition, a dream-like state, easy to dispel by questioning its reality.

The knowledge 'I am' is time bound, all your knowledge sprouts from the concept that you are. This infinitesimal seed contains the universe. You miss the point; you do not understand me properly. This principle 'I am' I am telling you about again and again. All questions will be over once you solve the riddle of 'I am'.

The knowledge 'I am' is within you with that conviction you worship. One who meditates on the knowledge, 'I am', everything in the realm of consciousness becomes clear to him. He lives without telling it, hence from this place, you carry the conviction about yourself that you know the knowledge 'I am' is God, there can be no other gain.

The knowledge 'I am' which is indwelling in you, worship that only.

The knowledge 'I am', and all its manifestations, are understood. In understanding, I am not that.

The knowledge 'I am', without memories and concepts, is everything. The idea 'I am the body and mind' is not that knowledge. No effort is required, the main thing is that 'you are' (or 'I am') when you listen to me and stay there, you'll understand that the knowledge 'I am' is independent of body-mind.

The Guru, God, and your own knowledge – these three are one. If you know that, you become quiet. Guru means knowledge and knowledge means 'I am'. The 'I amness' is itself the Guru.

The habit of considering the Self as body has influenced everybody too much.

The highest state is the state of a 'jnani'. The first step is to be that droplet ('I am'). In the process of knowing that droplet, you are out of it, and that is a 'jnani'. A 'jnani' is not obsessed by any calamities or any problems, because he has transcended the 'I am' principle. He watches the play as a witness.

The idea of responsibility is in your mind. You think there must be something or somebody solely responsible for all that happens. There is a contradiction between a multiple universe and a single cause. Either one or the other must be false. Or both. As I see it, it is all day-dreaming. There is no reality in ideas. The fact is that without you, neither the universe nor its cause could have come into being.

The impersonal is real, the personal appears and disappears. 'I am' is the impersonal being. 'I am this' is the person. The person is relative and the pure being – the fundamental.

The knowingness 'I am' is gradually felt by the child and this is followed by the mind. This 'I amness' or the feeling before the formation of the mind, is the ignorant-child-principle, termed the 'balkrishna' state. This 'balkrishna' principle has great potential. Here 'bal' means the food essence, child-body, and 'krishna' means 'non-knowing', that is, ignorance. But it has the potential to receive, respond and react. I am not in this state, the child principle, 'balkrishna', as I abide in the Absolute.

The knowledge 'I am' is a primary concept, and is also non-eternal. The One, the Absolute, which is eternal and aware, why should he worry about anybody else?

The knowledge 'I am' is not a thought but observes thought. The innermost, subtlest principle is that gnawing principle 'I am, I am' without words, by which you know you are. It has no form or image; it is only beingness, the love to be.

In that 'Parabrahman', which unconditioned, without attributes, without identity – the identity comes only when there is the knowledge 'I am' – so if that itself is not there, who is there to ask? This is to be understood not by 'someone' (with a body-mind identity), but it must be experienced, and in such a manner that the experiencer and experience are one.

The fragrance or sweetness of the food-essence body is the knowledge 'I am'. It has no name and form; it is the 'I love' state, the 'I-taste'. But from your body-mind state, you will go to pilgrimages and various gurus. So long as the consciousness is there, that humming goes on, and who does the humming? The principle which is humming and saying, 'I am, I am' is itself your guru.

The greatest appearance is the knowledge 'I am'. It is invisible before the birth and after the death of the body, and while it is visible it is a solid thing. Many great sages have appeared and disappeared because of the powerful seed 'I am'.

In that body the 'I am' is ticking – that is the Guru. You worship that 'I am' principle and surrender to that Guru and that Guru will give all the grace. What you call 'I am' and birth, you are not that, it is material. The Ultimate knowledge does not have any knowledge. This knowledge 'I am' has appeared spontaneously, as a result of the body. See it as it is, understand it as it is.

In that non-subjective state, the subject started. In the infinite state, the 'I am' state is temporary; don't give up your true standpoint otherwise you will be fooled. To whatever extent you would conduct your search, it would still be in the realm of 'I amness'. Don't retain it ('I am') in memory, then you will be happy.

The greatest guru is your inner self. Truly, he is the supreme teacher. He alone can take you to your goal and he alone meets you at the end of the road. Confide in him and you need no outer guru.

In the absence of beingness, when you did not know about your existence? Nothing was of any value to you. This memory 'I am' is neither true nor false; it is without these two attributes. That memory of beingness only appears to exist.

In the absence of these three states what do you think you are?

The Guru is the same all-pervading consciousness 'I am'. The SatGuru has gone beyond all these concepts, including the primary concept 'I am'.

The Guru tells you 'Get rid of concepts, just be yourself'. The seeker having understood what the Guru said gets rid of the concepts, and now, as the first step, the seeker dwells in the state 'I am', just being. First of all there is the knowingness 'I am', without words, with that knowingness the world is. Now when the seeker goes into meditation, that knowingness goes into no knowingness. This is the highest state in the hierarchy when the body aspect is there because this knowing and no-knowing are aspects of the body, and body means consciousness, and in the realm of consciousness, knowingness and no-knowingness exist. The Absolute transcends knowingness and no-knowingness. So, no-knowingness is the highest in the hierarchy of spirituality, and the destination is the transcendence of knowingness and no knowingness.

In the case of a devotee ('Bhakta'), initially the devotee does not want to leave God. Later on, even if the devotee asks God to go, God will not leave him. God means the knowledge 'I am'. The knowledge 'I am' is God ('Bhagwan').

In the body the indwelling principle is the consciousness. Abiding in the consciousness, it became all manifestation. Now transcendence of the consciousness has also occurred. With the appearance of consciousness, the Absolute knows it is, 'I am'. This is the experience. There are other experiences now, in this time factor, but experiences are gradually dropping off, including this primary experience 'I am'. It is only the consciousness that is going to disappear; the Absolute is always there.

In the body there is already that self-accomplished principle 'I am' which is witnessing mind and body, it is neither mind, body nor the vital breath. It has to be gradually realized that this principle has no form; it is subtler than the mind. By mistake the 'I am' accepts the body as itself, it is an exclusive principle apart from the body, mind and vital breath.

In the first few years the primary concept 'I am' was there, but in a dormant condition. Later on it started knowing itself. The 'jnani' state is like the child, when the child did not know itself. The apparatus through which that knowingness expresses itself is now quite different, but the principle is the same.

The eternal Absolute state of mine prior to the beingness, when the message 'I am' was not, is supremely significant. Who would have witnessed the message 'I am', if my priormost state of the 'nonbeingness' was not?

The fact is you. The only thing you know for sure is: 'here and now I am'. Remove the 'here and now', the 'I am' remains unassailable.

The feeling 'I am' is the quintessence of everything, but I the Absolute am not that. That 'I amness' is the highest knowledge. And this is surrendered here by the abidance in the action.

The first film is when that knowingness appears on you. In that knowledge 'I am' all is contained. Only in that film when the film started knowing itself, 'I am'; then you came to know all this. Did you know anything before?

The five elements disintegrate but I don't disappear. For instance, I am invited to some place to stay. The room in which I stay becomes my room, but does it belong to me? All belongs to the five elements. The essential contribution of the five elements is the 'I am' the five elements disintegrate, the 'I am' goes and a person is declared dead. Wherever I go to stay I always know my permanent abode.

In the immensity of consciousness a light appears, a tiny point that moves rapidly and traces shapes, thoughts and feelings, concepts and ideas, like a pen writing on paper. And the ink that leaves a trace is memory. You are that tiny point and by your movement the world is ever re-created. Stop moving and there will be no world. Look within and you will find that the point of light is the reflection of the immensity of light in the body as the sense 'I am'. There is only light all else appears.

In the mirror of your mind all kinds of pictures appear and disappear. Knowing that they are entirely your own creations, watch them silently come and go. Be alert, but not perturbed. This attitude of silent observation is the very foundation of yoga. You see the picture, but you are not the picture.

In the space, the movement starts with the air, the fire, the water, and the earth. All these five elements are you only. Out of your consciousness all this has happened. There is no individual. There is only you, the total functioning is you, the consciousness is you.

In the traditional view Brahman is supposed to have created the world, Vishnu to maintain it and Shiva to destroy it. Is not this Brahman who creates the world the same as the Brahma-randhra out of which the sense of 'I am' comes? Who is this Brahman other than the 'I amness'.

The deed is a fact, the doer a mere concept. Your very language shows that while the deed is certain, the doer is dubious; shifting responsibility is a game peculiarly human. Considering the endless list of factors required for anything to happen, one can only admit that everything is responsible for everything, however remote. Doership is a myth born from the illusion of "me" and "mine". I do not have the feeling that I am talking. There is talking going on, that is all. Do you [really talk]? You hear yourself talking and you say: I talk. I have no objections to the conventions of your language, but they distort and destroy reality. A more accurate way of saying would have been: "There is talking, working, coming, going". For anything to happen, the entire universe must coincide. It is wrong to believe that anything in particular can cause an event. Every cause is universal. Your very body would not exist without the entire universe contributing to its creation and survival. I am fully aware that things happen as they happen because the world is as it is. To affect the course of events, I must bring a new factor into the world and such factor can only be myself, the power of love and understanding focused in me.

In the waking state, the witnessing state is always there. There is no other Brahman greater than you, accept this and go, you are the greatest. In that small round cell is contained all the space, in it the Cosmos and earth are there, that small cell is the principle of 'I am' The moment it is there, space is manifested, the womb is space started from the small cell 'I am'.

The desire to find the self will be surely fulfilled, provided you want nothing else. But you must be honest with yourself and really want nothing else. If, in the meantime, you want many other things and are engaged in their pursuit, your main purpose may be delayed until you grow wiser and cease being torn between contradictory urges. Go within, without swerving, without ever looking outward.

In the womb that knowingness is ignorant of its existence, the 'I am' is not present but the 'I am' principle is started there. All things happen unknowingly, but even to understand that is very difficult, it is beyond our comprehension.

The dissolution of personality is followed always by a sense of great relief, as if a heavy burden has fallen off.

The emergence of this beingness itself constitutes time. Everything is beingness, but I, the Absolute, am not that. In meditation there was space, when suddenly two forms appeared out of no-form, 'Prakriti' and 'Purusha' and the quintessence of these forms was the knowledge 'I am'.

The entire manifestation of your world and universe is just the expression and manifestation of your Beingness.

In this body is the subtle principle 'I am', that principle witnesses all this. You are not the words. Words are the expression of space, they are not yours. Still further you are not that 'I am'.

The confidence and knowledge that 'you are', on what does it depend? Beingness becomes no beingness and no-beingness spontaneously becomes beingness, so whom should we question? You should yourself investigate it; what is the support of the 'I am'? On what does the faith that 'you are' depend? Why is there beingness? Why am I? How am I? People only think of the body and mind, then, come death and the faith 'I am' disappears.

In this process you, as an individual, are not left at all. Try to understand that 'I am' is a product of the 'satwa guna', food essence product. When you throw out all the concepts, including your primary concept ('I am'), then whatever is, is. Stay put in quietude.

In this spiritual hierarchy, from the grossest to the subtlest, you are the subtlest. How can this be realized? The very base is that you don't know you are, and suddenly the feeling of 'I amness' appears. The moment it appears you see space, mental space; that subtle sky-like space, stabilize there. You are that. When you are able to stabilize in that space, you are space only. When this spacelike identity 'I am' disappears, the space will also disappear, there is no space. When that space-like 'I am' goes into oblivion, that is the eternal state, 'nirguna', no form, no beingness. Actually, what did happen there? This message 'I am' was no message. Dealing with this aspect, I cannot talk much because there is no scope to put it in words.

The consciousness that 'I am' has created, and sustains, all the wonders in the world for which men take credit; on the other hand this consciousness has no control over itself. The principle out of which you have sprouted has tremendous powers. Lord Krishna has said, 'You worship me, be devoted to me', this means what?

The consciousness that has come out of the five elements, through the body, is the quality of beingness, the knowledge that 'I am'. That state of beingness will perish. There is no necessity for following any particular path, everything is the same. Think of that which is the center of the cosmos; don't let your attention stray in any way from the knowledge of beingness, 'I am'. Keep on knowing that 'I am' and through this insistence you will know the state you want to reach.

Increase and widen your desires till nothing but reality can fulfil them. It is not desire that is wrong, but its narrowness and smallness. Desire is devotion. By all means be devoted to the real , the infinite, the eternal heart of being. Your longing to be happy is there. Why? Because you love yourself. By all means, love yourself -wisely. What is wrong is to love yourself stupidly, so as to make yourself suffer. Love yourself wisely. Both indulgence and austerity have the same purpose in view - to make you happy. Indulgence is the stupid way, austerity is the wise way. Once you have gone through an experience, not to go through it again is austerity. To eschew the unnecessary is austerity. Not to anticipate pleasure or pain is austerity. Having things under control at all times is austerity. Desire by itself is not wrong. It is the choices that you make that are wrong. To imagine that some little thing - food, sex, power, fame - will make you happy is to deceive yourself. Only something as vast and deep as your real self can make you truly and lastingly happy.

The core of this consciousness is knowingness, to know 'I am'. It is not a personality, not an individual. It is total manifestation. Beingness is there, it fills everything. Nevertheless, this quality 'I am' is the result of the material, objective body. In the seed the whole tree is latent. In the droplet 'I am' all three worlds are squeezed in.

Increase the conviction that you are the formless consciousness. You develop your firm conviction that you are the total manifesting universal consciousness. There is nobody who can have the knowledge of the Truth, the Eternal. It is one's eternal true state, but is not a knowledgeable state – you cannot know It. So-called knowledge is boundless and plenty in the state of attributes, 'I am'. In this body is the knowledge 'I am'. When the body drops down, the knowledge 'I am' will subside there only – what remains is the Absolute.

Intelligence is innately there like fire in the match stick. The final culmination of the elemental interplay is the human body, where the touch of 'I am' appears. Birth is like a spark coming from the rubbing of stones, there is the elemental friction and you have the spark 'I am'. The qualities of a Bodhisattva are due to the knowledge 'I am', but that is temporary and so the perfect Jnani says all manifestation is unreal, only 'Parabrahman' is real.

Investigate that concept 'I am.' In the process of trying to find out your identity or this spiritual search, all will happen in the realm of this consciousness. You finally stumble on, or culminate into the Absolute 'Parabrahman' state, which is desireless.

The capacity of consciousness is something astounding. I didn't know I was, and then suddenly I knew 'I am'. This 'I amness' is the power of 'Maya'.

The capital we have is the knowledge 'I am'. But what have we done? We have handed over that knowledge to the body and we say 'I am the body'. Thereby we have reduced the totality, the limitless, to the limited – a specified insignificant body. And that is why, being unable to give up this association with the body, we are afraid of dying.

The child has been given an idea who its parents are, but is just a concept. Similarly the 'I am' is just a concept. The child has been given the idea that 'He is'. First you must investigate 'Who is' and what this 'I amness' is. You want to know what the support is for the 'I am'? My parents supported me! When do these two people, the husband and the wife become parents? It's when a child is born, is that not true? Where are the parents before the birth of the child? And what is the child? The child is the root of parents; the child is also the father of the parents. Because of the child the parents are. This shows how completely hollow our egos are.

Is it necessary that you should remember that you are ('I am')? Spontaneously you know and remember that you are. That is why you have come here, have you not? It is because you are. Stay put there.

The concentration on 'I am' is a form of attention. Give your undivided attention to the most important thing in your life – yourself. Of your personal universe you are the center – without knowing the center what else can you know?

The concept 'I am' is the primordial 'maya'. And that 'maya', that primordial concept 'I am' requires support and therefore God.

It is prior to the 'I am', it's the unborn state, so how can it have or even require the knowledge 'I am'?

Is there a world outside your knowledge? Can you go beyond what you know? You may postulate a world beyond the mind, but it will remain a concept, unproved and unprovable. Your experience is your proof, and it is valid for you only. Who else can have your experience, when the other person is only as real as he appears in your experience?

It [dying] needn't be so [painful and ugly]. It may be beautiful and peaceful. Once you know that death happens to the body and not to you, you just watch your body falling off like a discarded garment. Once you know that the body alone dies and not the continuity of memory and the sense of "I am" reflected in it, you are afraid no longer.

The body dies. This means what? It means only the thought 'I am', that concept, has disappeared. Nothing has happened to the knower of the whole happening. So long as the basic concept 'I am' is there, the conceptual element cannot disappear. It is the concept itself that has given various names to itself, but it is still the same concept. Before this concept of 'I am' came on you, were you happy or unhappy? Was there even any feeling of happiness or unhappiness or any of the dualities? In the absence of the basic concept 'I am', there is no thought, no awareness, and no consciousness of one's existence.

The body falls down but what happened to me? For that principle for which you get no reply, is perfect, whatever answer you get is wrong. If I think of this world, why should I not inquire about prior to consciousness? If I tackle this question, I must investigate what is this principle of 'I am'? I would prefer to play with that child not born because eternal Parabraman and unborn children are alike.

The body identity cannot get this knowledge, the knowledge 'I am' must get this knowledge 'I am', when knowledge abides in knowledge there is transcendence of knowledge.

The body identity cannot get this knowledge, the knowledge 'I am' must get this knowledge; when knowledge abides in knowledge there is transcendence of knowledge.

The body is not you, the name is not you. The body is the food you have consumed; the taste of it is the knowledge 'I am'. That is Self, the feeling 'I am', that is the love to be. How amazing, how incredible, it has no name, but you give many names to it. It is the Self, the love to be. That love to be is all pervading. Before you conceptualize anything, you are, even before the knowingness, you are.

It [the dream] appears to be beginningless, but in fact it is only now. From moment to moment you are renewing it. Once you have seen that you are dreaming, you shall wake up. But you do not see because you want the dream to continue. A day will come when you will long for the ending of the dream, with all your heart and mind, and be willing to pay the price; the price will be dispassion and detachment, the loss of interest in the dream itself. Wanting it to continue is not inevitable. See clearly your condition, your very clarity will release you.

It has nothing to do with effort. Just turn away, look between the thoughts, rather than at the thoughts. When you happen to walk in a crowd, you do not fight every man you meet, you just find your way between. When you fight, you invite a fight. But when you do not resist, you meet no resistance. When you refuse to play the game, you are out of it.

The beginning and the end of knowledge is the 'I am', be attentive to the 'I am', once you understand it, you are apart from it.

It is because the 'I am' is false that it wants to continue. Reality need not continue – knowing itself indestructible, it is indifferent to the destruction of forms and expressions. To strengthen and stabilize the 'I am' we do all sorts of things – all in vain for the 'I am' is being rebuilt from moment to moment. No ambition is spiritual. All ambitions are for the sake of 'I am'. If you want to make real progress you must give up all ideas of personal attainment.

It is like washing printed cloth. First the design fades, then the background, and in the end the cloth is plain white. The personality gives place to the witness, then the witness goes and pure awareness remains. The cloth was white in the beginning and is white in the end; the patterns and colors just happened for a time.

The beingness, the 'I am', is merely an instrument, it is not you. It is an instrument of knowledge, and that great instrument of knowledge is called God, which is the quality of the food essence. Out of that alone you will be able to see everything else.

The best is the simple feeling 'I am'. Dwell on it patiently. Here patience is wisdom; don't think of failure. There can be no failure in this undertaking.

The Bhagavad-Gita says that we have five senses of knowledge; these are very subtle. More subtle than the senses is the mind, subtler than the mind is the intelligence, and subtler than these is the vital breath. And yet more subtle is 'He', the beingness, the 'I am'.

It is not important where you are, once you are established in the 'I am'. It is like space – it neither comes nor goes; just as when you demolish the walls of a building only space remains.

It is not what you do, but what you stop doing that matters.

It is only during the duration of the beingness that the world and creation is. This power is the faith in the primordial concept 'I am', and that is the concept that weaves the web of creation. The entire manifestation is an appearance in this concept.

It is pure awareness that knows 'I am'. Who can understand that illusory state? 'I amness' is illusory only. It is not a perfect state, it is illusion. Who knows the illusion? A non-illusory state only can know the illusory state. But what is the necessity to say pure awareness? 'Awareness' means pure. Since awareness knows 'I am', it is other; it is more than 'I am'. That is the highest; there are no gradations in awareness. In the Absolute, the 'Parabrahman' state, there is no question of impure or pure awareness.

The active part is called Maya, and is due to the mind. The inactive part is called 'I amness' or Purusha, which is just watching. Only when you identify with that which is stationary, the Purusha, can you become the watcher of the 'I amness' and all of its activities.

The aim is to awaken yourself to the faith in the self, 'I am'. That is the entire purpose. So whatever is inductive to that development, you may accept. Suppose you have faith in a living guru, then, accept a living guru. If you have faith in a guru who has left his body, accept that guru.

The appearance of the primary concept 'I am' is the beginning of duality. I started counting with myself, before this counting starts. That has no number. That is the Absolute. With that little movement 'I am' this counting started.

It is right to say 'I am', but to say 'I am this', 'I am that', is a sign of not enquiring, not examining, of mental weakness or lethargy. Practice (sadhana) consists of reminding oneself forcibly of one's pure 'beingness', of not being anything in particular, not a sum of particulars, not even the totality of all particulars, which make up a universe.

The Atman has no birth, this touch of 'I am' is a hoarding of the Absolute, and only the advertisement disappears. The 'I am' is an illusion, temporary; the one who knows this knows the eternal principle. Whatever experiences you enjoy are an imperfect state. You involve yourself in practices, because the mind does not let you be quiet.

The atomic consciousness contains the whole Universe, but yet he (the 'jnani') knows that he is not that consciousness. So in that case what pride can he have? He is the Absolute state, in which the 'I am' consciousness is absent. If you meet any 'jnanis, you will find it easy to recognize them, for they will not have any pride in their Self-knowledge, since they have transcended that knowledge also. They say 'I am not this knowledge or this consciousness'.

It is the 'I am' that investigates the 'I am' and on realizing its falsehood it disappears and merges into eternity.

It is the absolute in you that takes you to the absolute beyond you - absolute truth, love, selflessness are the decisive factors in self-realization. With earnestness these can be reached.

It is the person you imagine yourself to be that suffers, not you. Dissolve it in awareness. It is merely a bundle of memories and habits. From the awareness of the unreal to the awareness of your real nature there is a chasm which you will easily cross, once you have mastered the art of pure awareness.

It is very simple. The body and in the body…it is like a coin. On one side, you have the vital breath for making possible all activity; and on the other side is the knowledge 'I am'. Only when the vital breath is there, the knowledge 'I am' is present. When the vital breath leaves the body, the knowledge 'I am' also disappears. And both of these are the product of the food essence body. I am not that; this entire composite I am not. This you have to realize.

The 'mumukshu, is in kindergarten, spiritually inclined, but identifying with the body-mind. The 'sadhaka' is one who has disidentified with the body-mind. A 'siddha' is one who has stabilized in the knowledge 'I am', and in the process, has transcended it. In this journey you very well know where you are.

The 'sadhana', the discipline, is only this: The knowledge which is dwelling in this body, the quintessence of these three 'gunas' – the knowledge 'I am', 'I am that' – this is the initial step. You must be one with it; you must abide in that only. You have to think 'I am not the body but I am that formless, nameless knowledge indwelling in this body'; that (is) 'I am'. When you abide sufficiently long in this state, whatever doubts you may have, that knowledge 'I am' itself will sprout out with life and meaning for you, intended for you only, and everything will become clear. No external knowledge will be necessary.

The 'So Hum' Japa is incessantly going on in your pulse, indicating 'I am' get in tune with it by recitation. That 'So Hum' energy without words is the raw material of incarnations and the incarnations are the hoardings of the primary principle. The primordial principle is 'Parabrahman'; its advertisement is done by movement, the stirrings of 'So Hum'. By its movement it is praising the primordial principle, that advertising material is the 'Moolmaya' (Primary Illusion). That incarnating principle – the 'Moolmaya'– gives knowledge to the incarnated.

The Absolute is watching this 'I amness' that is sustained by the food body. Is it clear? After some time passes in the waking state, rest is required, so the 'I amness' goes into oblivion. It goes to rest and forgets itself. You may not comprehend exactly what it means now, but as you get established in the Beingness you will understand how.

The Absolute state does not know itself, but the Absolute is offered and opportunity to understand itself through the food product.

Just as every drop of the ocean carries the taste of the ocean, so does every moment carry the taste of eternity. Definitions and descriptions have their place as useful incentives for further search, but you must go beyond them into what is undefinable and indescribable, except in negative terms.

Just as the salty taste is present in the entire ocean, the beingness or the sense of 'I am' in the human form has the inherent capacity to be all-pervading, but having being conditioned – and thereby limited – itself to the body form, it is interested only in protecting and preserving the body.

Just keep in mind the feeling "I am", merge in it, till your mind and feeling become one. By repeated attempts, you will stumble on the right balance of attention and affection, and your mind will be firmly established in the thought-feeling "I am". Whatever you think, say or do, this sense of immutable and affectionate being remains as the ever-present background of the mind.

The 'I am' means all this spectacle that you are seeing, later, you also see that number of universes are playing in that 'I am'. When you understand all this verbally, you may become a pseudo-Guru, which is not realization. You must realize that you only observe, and you are not that, you are not that 'I am' in which universes are playing.

The 'I amness' is pulsating 'I am, I am'. The feeling of 'I amness' is there because of the essence of the food body and vital breath, when these are gone the pulsation of 'I amness' will not be there. Beingness goes into no-beingness.

Just sit and know that 'you are' the 'I am' without words, nothing else has to be done; shortly you will arrive to your natural Absolute state.

Just be 'you are'. Do you follow?

Just try to be in that 'I amness' don't try to put effort and concentration When 'you are' it is 'I amness', when 'you are' the beingness is automatically there. Whatever 'you are' without doing any effort, be there. Don't try to interpret 'I amness'. You are without the body sense, when you identify with body-mind, then the trouble begins

The 'Linga-deha' is the seed, the chemical, the product of the five elemental essences which give rise to and sustain the consciousness 'I am'. Just like the seed of a tree, that seed latently contains all future manifestations and expressions of the tree that will sprout out of the seed. You take a fountain pen and on the paper you put a drop of ink, so that drop is the 'Linga-deha'. That drop is the moment of conception; its expression is the thoughtfree state, like space, in the knowingness state. That 'Linga-deha', that little drop, and the knowledge 'I am' is the same.

Just turn away from all that occupies the mind; do whatever work you have to complete, but avoid new obligations; keep empty, keep available, resist not what comes uninvited. In the end, you reach a state of non-grasping, of joyful non-attachment, of inner ease and freedom indescribable, yet wonderfully real.

The 'I amness' together with the vital breath appear spontaneously when the body is created. The vital breath and food body are necessary to sustain the 'I amness'. When the food body is dropped by the vital breath the 'I amness' disappears. Where does the flame go when it is extinguished? The same thing applies to the 'I amness'.

The 'Maya' is so powerful that it gets you completely wrapped up in it. 'Maya' means 'I am', 'I love to be'. It has no identity except love. That knowledge of 'I am' is the greatest foe and the greatest friend. Although it might be your greatest enemy, if you propitiate it properly, it will turn around and lead you to the highest state.

The 'I am' is the sum total of all that you perceive, it's time-bound, the 'I am' itself is an illusion, you are not the 'I am' you are prior to it.

The 'I am' is the sum total of everything you perceive. It appears spontaneously and disappears, it has no dwelling place. It is like a dream world. Do not try to be something, even a spiritual person. You are the manifested. The tree is already there in the seed. Such is the 'I am'. Just see it as it is.

The 'I am' is there throughout his or her life even if a person lives for a hundred years, but the 'I am' disappears when the body is gone. This is called death.

The 'I am' and the Absolute are not two. In the Absolute the 'I amness' comes and then the experience takes place. Whatever is happening, from the Absolute standpoint, without the knowledge 'I am', is very profound, unlimited, and expansive

The 'I am' connotes the three states, waking, dream and deep sleep. 'I am' means that you are these three states, when these are gone the memory is also gone.

The 'I am' consciousness is the advertisement of The Absolute. The Absolute is unknown, what you call Ishwara, Brahma and so forth are hoardings of The Absolute.

The 'I am' has great potency, the entire manifestation has come from it. When you dwell in the 'I am' as your destiny you realize that your destiny is not death but the disappearance of 'I am'.

The 'I am' in a child is dormant, it does not know itself, but it is there, in due course it knows itself and as a one knows 'I am'. Go to the root, the beginning of the child, when you understand that you are not consciousness, stabilize there; understand and get out.

The 'I am' in body form can reach the highest state only if you understand, accept it and dwell there. Then you escape birth and death.

The 'I am' is a thought, while awareness is not a thought; there is no 'I am aware' in awareness. Consciousness is an attribute while awareness is not, one can be aware of being conscious, but not conscious of awareness. God is the totality of consciousness, but awareness is beyond all – being as well as non-being.

The 'I am' is a useful pointer; it shows where to seek, but not what to seek. Just have a good look at it. Once you are convinced that you cannot say truthfully about yourself anything except 'I am', and that nothing can be pointed at, can be yourself, the need for the 'I am' is over- you are no longer intent on verbalizing what you are. All definitions apply to your body only and to its expressions. Once this obsession with the body goes, you will revert to your natural state. We discover the natural state by being earnest, by searching, enquiring, questioning daily and hourly, by giving one's life to this discovery.

The 'I am' is absent only in the state of 'samadhi', when the self merges in the Self. Otherwise it will be there. In the state of a realized person the 'I am' is there, he just doesn't give much importance to it. A 'jnani' is not guided by a concept.

The 'I am' is all, the God, just know that the 'I am' is God, this is the first step, the knowledge 'I am' is yourself. All other activities will follow; you just get established in the knowledge. 'I am', it is the sun, and all other activities are rays

The 'I am' is at the root of all appearance and the permanent link in the succession of events that we call life; but I am beyond the 'I am'.

The 'I am' is in a dormant condition in the womb, it is an ignorant condition. How could it know itself? At three years or so the knowledge 'I am' comes spontaneously with the formation of body. Around middle age it is at a climax, while in old age the quality of 'I amness' is diminished. Then finally the 'I am' disappears, and identity too is gone.

The 'I am' is objective, it is the 'I am' that investigates and it is the 'I am' that disposes itself off and stabilizes in Eternity. The body is made up of elements; the quintessence or quality (guna) is the 'I am'. You replenish the food-body or 'I amness' with water and food.

The 'I am' is sustained by the food body, that is, our body, which is the food for the 'I am'. Every creature depends on its food and the 'I am' depends upon our body. Will you remember this?

The 'I am' is the center or the essence of the food body, which is a result of the five elements. Out of spacial activity there is water, vegetation and so forth, so 'I amness' is a culmination of the five elemental activity. This 'I amness', whenever enjoyed beyond the body is your destiny. When you dwell in destiny as 'I am', you realize that it is not your death, but the disappearance of 'I amness.' You just dwell in it, and itself it will tell you its own story.

The 'I am' is the only God to be pleased. Whatever you presently know about God is only bargaining. Your very existence or beingness is the proof that God exists. If I am not, God is not. God's existence is due to the consciousness, the 'I am', please it and it will lead you to its source.

Keep focused on the 'I am' till you become a witness to it, then you stand apart, you have reached the highest.

Keep quiet. Do your work in the world, but inwardly keep quiet. Then all will come to you. Do not rely on your work for realization. It may profit others, but not you. Your hope lies in keeping silent in your mind and quiet in your heart. Realized people are very quiet.

That principle 'I am' is your illusion but the Oneness got rid of that illusion. Then one is without body or mind. The principle of Oneness has no shape, therefore male and female have no shape – this is the wedding of the male and female. At that stage the barren women conceived and progeny is delivered! That is the 'I am' state and that is the universe. But this Oneness is not a state of illusion.

That state in which you were before you acquired this knowledge 'I am' is the real state. Only after you got this knowledge you identified with the body-mind. Whatever you have acquired, including the body-mind, that will go, and it is useless, and that is that. But your original state, before you acquired the body, is the Truth, is the Real state, and it will remain.

Keep the 'I am' in the focus of awareness, remember that you 'are', watch yourself ceaselessly and the unconscious will flow into the conscious without any special effort on your part. The person merges into the witness, the witness into awareness, awareness into pure being, yet identity is not lost, only its limitations are lost. It is transfigured and becomes the real Self, the 'sadguru', the eternal friend and guide. To go deeper, meditation is essential, the striving to go beyond the states of sleep, dream and waking. In the beginning the attempts are irregular, then recur more often, become regular, then continuous and intense, until all obstacles are conquered.

Keep very quiet and watch what comes to the surface of the mind. Reject the known, welcome the so far unknown and reject it in its turn. Thus you come to a state in which there is no knowledge, only being, in which being itself is knowledge. To know by being is direct knowledge. It is based on the identity of the seer and the seen. Indirect knowledge is based on sensation and memory, on proximity of the perceiver and his percept, confined with the contrast between the two.

That state of being is common to all, which is the message 'I am' without words. Change is only in the mind-flow. All the studies you are doing are in the realm of mind-flow. The sense of 'I am' is present because of your birth, through which you encounter many thoughts and concepts, always changing. Presently the message 'I am' is constant.

That ultimate state is known as 'vishranti', which means total rest, complete relaxation, utter quietude etc. The other meaning, by splitting the word, would be, 'vishara (visra)-anti' – forget yourself in the end. That means in the ultimate state, 'you-are-ness' is totally forgotten. Whether 'I am' or 'I am not' both are forgotten. This is the highest type of rest – 'parama-vishranti'.

That which you like most – is the 'I am', the conscious presence – but that is not going to last forever. When the body drops off and the consciousness is extinguished, you need to do nothing. With this understanding do what you like in the world.

Knowing that you are not the body, watch the vital breath as a flow of the mind. You are here in the spark of 'I amness'. When you acknowledge the 'I amness' you become the spark. I am like space and do not have an identity – this is my 'I amness' from which all the talk is being produced.

Look at the 'I am' as a sign of love between the inner and the outer, the real and the appearance. Just like in a dream all is different, except the sense of 'I', which enables you to say 'I dreamt', so does the sense of 'I am' enable you to say, 'I am my real Self again. I do nothing nor is anything done to me. I am what I am and nothing can affect me. I appear to depend on everything, but in fact all depends on me'.

Look at yourself steadily – it is enough. The door that locks you in is also the door that lets you out. The 'I am' is the door. Stay at it until it opens. As a matter of fact, it is open, only you are not at it. You are waiting at the non-existent painted doors, which will never open.

Look closely and you will see that the seer and the seen appear only when there is seeing. They are attributes of seeing. When you say "I am seeing this", "I am" and "this" come with the seeing, nor before. You cannot have an unseen "this" nor an unseeing "I am". Knowing is a reflection of your true nature along with being and loving. The knower and the known are added by the mind. It is in the nature of the mind to create a subject-object duality, where there is none.

That attention of 'I amness' is always there in the waking state, but we are not alert to watch it. There is no other attention to be followed. Be attentive to that attention 'I am'.

That feeling of love must be understood and then love will unfold itself. Love for the Self, this consciousness, 'I am', those who have understood this as the true love, have themselves become love. All has merged in them.

Lord Krishna said 'All are my expressions'. This knowledge 'I am' in each species is myself. The very life force – luminous, bright, radiant, indwelling principle is myself.

Love is not selective, desire is selective. In love there are no strangers.

That knowingness alone points out all the dirt which is imposed on it. Even the space is not as pure as the knowledge 'I am'. Innately the world is very pure; it is rendered dirty because you identify with the body. Since you do not recognize your 'I amness' in its purity, you refer to various books and saints to get an identity.

That knowledge 'I am' is born out of love, but the illusion has taken such hold of it that love for the 'I amness' has gone into the background. To stay with it has become increasingly difficult. Without the manifestation the love was total.

Meditation is a deliberate attempt to pierce into the higher states of consciousness and finally go beyond it. The art of meditation is the art of shifting the focus of attention to ever subtler levels, without losing one's grip on the levels left behind. The final stage of meditation is reached when the sense of identity goes beyond the "I-am-so-and-so", beyond "so-I-am", beyond "I-am-the-witness-only", beyond "there-is", beyond all ideas into the impersonally personal pure being. But you must be energetic when you take to meditation. It is definitely not a part-time occupation. Limit your interests and activities to what is needed for you and your dependents' barest needs. Save all your energies and time for breaking the wall your mind had built around you. Believe me, you will not regret.

Stop making use of your mind and see what happens. Do this one thing thoroughly. That is all.

That love, that knowledge which gives light is the knowledge 'I am'. Focus on your beingness until you become established in it. Only then will you be able to transcend it. Your focus at present is on air or the breath (addressed to the one doing Pranayama). 'Be' that beingness, though, this also is not the final step.

Manifested Brahma is the 'I am', whatever principle is prior to the utterance of sound, that principle proclaims by itself. What I insists is that you must stabilize is that state. The recitation of the mantra 'So Hum' must be for a very long time, it is prior to words. When that 'So Hum' principle, is pleased, that principle, represented by these words, expounds knowledge.

Maya is the primary source of illusion. At that point, love for the Self begins: 'I am', the love to be. Its expression is all this manifestation.

Suppose a question is asked of you, what were you a hundred years back? You would reply 'I was not'. That means, I was not like 'this', that is not like this present 'I am'. Who (and how) could (he) say 'I was not like this'? The one who says this, was he not there? The one who was prior to a hundred years was not like this present 'I am', but he was and is now.

Take it that you are That. 'That' means no shape, no design.

That (Absolute) state is not to be experienced, about that you can't speak. Just be that state, what is experienced is not truth. What is experienced is not truth that is the primary problem. I did not know that I was in that state, suddenly I knew, 'I am', thus all the trouble. In that state there was no knowingness, suddenly 'I am' and I caught hold of the body. My identity of 'I amness' is the entire manifestation, not individual body. All the trouble began with the 'otherness', a quality that came with 'I amness'.

That 'I am' is a concept, is to be understood while the concept is there. Once it merges in the original state, who (or what) is there who wants to know? The illusory entity has disappeared.

Meditation will help you to find your bonds, loosen them, untie them and cast your moorings. When you are no longer attached to anything, you have done your share. The rest will be done for you.

Most essential is that knowledge 'I am'. Claim it; appropriate it as your own. If that is not there, nothing is. Knowledge of all stages will be obtained only with the aid of this knowledge 'I am' From the Absolute no-knowing state, spontaneously this consciousness 'I am' has appeared – no reason, no cause.

Most of your experiences are unconscious. The conscious ones are very few. You are unaware of the fact because to you only the conscious ones count. Become aware of the unconscious. Desire and fear are the obscuring and distorting factors. When mind is free of them the unconscious becomes accessible.

My advice to you is very simple – just remember yourself, 'I am', it is enough to heal your mind and take you beyond, just have some trust. I don't mislead you. Why should I? Do I want anything from you? I wish you well – such is my nature. Why should I mislead you? Commonsense too will tell you that to fulfill a desire you must keep your mind on it. If you want to know your true nature, you must have yourself in mind all the time, until the secret of your being stands revealed.

My feeling is that all that happens in space and time happens to me, that every experience is my experience, every form is my form. What I take myself to be becomes my body, and all that happens to that body becomes my mind. But at the root of the universe there is pure awareness, beyond space and time, here and now. Know it to be your real being and act accordingly.

My guru further pointed out to me the fact that the only thing you have and which you can utilize to unravel the mystery of life, is this knowledge 'I am'. Without that there is absolutely nothing, so I got hold of it, as my guru advised me, and then I wanted to find out how the spiritual aspect of 'me' came about without my knowledge. On my pure Absoluteness, which has no place, and no shape or form, this knowledge 'I am' came, which also has no shape or form. Therefore, it appears; and it is only an illusion.

My Guru pointed out to me that originally I had nothing to do with all this and all I have with which to solve this mystery of life is the knowledge 'I am'; without that there is nothing. So I got hold of it, as my Guru told me, and then I wanted to find out how this body aspect came about without my knowledge and how alone on that any other knowledge come about, and that again is a result of five elements. Therefore, whatever anybody thinks he has, is sheer ignorance, and I know it from my own experience.

My Guru taught me what 'I am', I pondered only on that. My consciousness appeared along with my body form. My original state is to be in that state where there is no 'I am'. I am explaining my state of affairs, from my standpoint you must realize yourself.

My Guru told me 'Divinity' (Paramatman) is what you are', I heard it and I accepted it, I did not want to gain anything, I just accepted it. I never knew that 'I' existed and suddenly I was aware that 'I am' this Absolute Truth. I had complete faith in the words of my Guru and then later on everything happened spontaneously.

Something prevents you from seeing that there is nothing you need. Find it out and see its falseness. It is like having swallowed some poison and suffering from unquenchable craving for water. Instead of drinking beyond all measure, why not eliminate the poison and be free of this burning thirst? The sense "I am a person in time and space" is the poison. In a way, time itself is the poison. In time all things come to an end and new are born, to be devoured in their turn. Do not identify yourself with time, do not ask anxiously "what next, what next?" Step out of time and see it devour the world. Say: "Well, it is in the nature of time to put an end to everything. Let it be. It does not concern me. I am not combustible, nor do I need to collect fuel."

Source is the real thing. As you progress and get established in Beingness you will understand that you are above the dreaming and waking states, as these pertain only to your 'I amness'. When the 'I amness' is not there, the tool required to observe is also not there. Once there is Self-realization, the whole riddle is solved.

Start with the body. From the body you get the knowledge 'I am'. In this process you become more and more subtle. When you are in a position to witness the knowledge 'I am', you have reached the highest. In this way you must try to understand, and the seeds of knowledge will sprout in you.

Stay without ambition, without the least desire, exposed, vulnerable, unprotected, uncertain and alone, completely open to and welcoming life as it happens, without the selfish conviction that all must yield you pleasure or profit, material or so-called spiritual.

My statement, and that of my guru, is that childhood is a cheat, it is false. The knowledge 'I am' itself is a cheat. When the beingness appears, that love for existence is a result of the primary illusion, that 'maya'. Once you come to know that you exist, you feel like enduring eternally, you always want to be, to exist, to survive. And so the struggle begins, all because of 'maya'.

My teacher told me to hold on to the sense 'I am' tenaciously and not to swerve from it even for a moment. I did my best to follow his advice and in a comparatively short time I realized within myself the truth of his teaching. All I did was to remember his teaching, his face, his words constantly. This brought an end to the mind, in the stillness of the mind I saw myself as I am – unbound.

Nature is neither pleasant nor painful. It is all intelligence and beauty. Pain and pleasure are in the mind. Change your scale of values and all will change. Pleasure and pain are mere disturbances of the senses; treat them equally and there will be only bliss. And the world is what you make it; by all means, make it happy. Only contentment can make you happy, desires fulfilled breed more desires. Keeping away from all desires and contentment in what comes by itself is a very fruitful state, a precondition to the state of fullness. Don't distrust its apparent sterility and emptiness. Believe me, it is the satisfaction of desires that breeds misery. Freedom from desires is bliss.

Selfishness is the cause of suffering. There is no other cause. It is only with separateness and self-seeking that real suffering appears in the world.

Self-remembrance, awareness of "I am' ripens man powerfully and speedily. Give up all ideas about yourself and simply be. Stop making use of your mind and see what happens. Do this one thing thoroughly. That is all.

Shall we call the knowledge 'I am' the guru? But even that knowledge you are not! Knowledge 'I am' means consciousness, God, 'Ishwara', guru etc. but you the Absolute are not that.

Since everything is 'You', you can't cut it away from you. This knowledge of 'I amness' is part of you. How can you throw it away? And where can you throw it?

Sitting quietly, being one with the knowledge 'I am', you will lose all concern with the world, then the 'I am' will also go, leaving you as the Absolute.

So long as the concept 'I am' is still there, they (people who contact maharaj) have not gone beyond or prior to it; they have not gone beyond the total manifestation. So now when people come here, I talk with them, from what level am I talking? I am talking from the level that you are consciousness and not the body-mind. In my state whatever comes out is from the total manifestation, not from the point of view of the Absolute. Hang on to that consciousness, which is your only capital, and do 'dhyana' and let that unfold whatever knowledge has to be unfolded.

Neither ignorance nor illusion ever happened to you. Find the self to which you ascribe ignorance and illusion and your question will be answered. You talk as if you know the self and see it to be under the sway of ignorance and illusion. But, in fact, you do not know the self, nor are you aware of ignorance. By all means, become aware, this will bring you to the self and you will realize that there is neither ignorance nor delusion in it. It is like saying: if there is sun, how can darkness be? As under a stone there will be darkness, however strong the sunlight, so in the shadow of the "I-am-the-body" consciousness there must be ignorance and illusion. Don't ask 'why' and 'how'. It is in the nature of creative imagination to identify itself with its creations. You can stop it any moment by switching off attention. Or though investigation.

No use rebelling against the very pattern of life. If you seek the immutable, go beyond experience. When I say remember 'I am' all the time, I mean come back to it repeatedly. No particular thought can be mind's natural state, only silence. Not the idea of silence but silence itself. When the mind is in its natural state, it reverts to silence spontaneously after every experience, or rather, every experience happens against a background of silence. Now, what you have learnt here becomes the seed. You may forget it – apparently. But it will live and in due season sprout and grow and bring forth flowers and fruits. All will happen by itself. You need not do anything, only don't prevent it.

No way to self-realization is short or long, but some people are more in earnest and some are less. I can tell you about myself. I was a simple man, but I trusted my Guru. What he told me to do, I did. He told me to concentrate on 'I am' – I did. He told me that I am beyond all perceivables and conceivables – I believed. I gave my heart and soul, my entire attention and the whole of my spare time (I had to work to keep my family alive). As a result of faith and earnest application, I realized my self ('swarupa') within three years. You may choose any way that suits you; your earnestness will determine the rate of progress. Establish yourself firmly in the awareness of 'I am'. This is the beginning and also the end of all endeavor.

Seek liberation by seeing that one self is not anything personal or perceivable.

Self it is absolutely happy but after the child is two or three years old, gradually it gets involved in 'I' and 'mine', and gradually he loses hold of the joy 'I am'. The result of this involvement is that he comes to the conclusion that he was born and is going to die.

Self-identification with the body creates ever fresh desires, and there is no end to them, unless this mechanism of bondage is clearly seen. It is clarity that is liberating, for you cannot abandon desire unless its causes and effects are clearly seen.

Self-identification with the body-mind is the poison that brings bondage.

Self-interest and self-concern are the focal points of the false. Your daily life vibrates between desire and fear. Watch it intently and you will see how the mind assumes innumerable names and shapes, like a river foaming between the boulders. Trace every action to its selfish motive and look at the motive intently till it dissolves. Discard every self-seeking motive as soon as it is seen and you need not look for truth; truth will find you.

Nobody can compel another to live. Besides, there were cultures in which suicide had its acknowledged and respected place. There is noble virtue in unshakable endurance of whatever comes, but there is also dignity in the refusal of meaningless torture and humiliation.

Normally in the name of spirituality, knowledge is expounded. Knowledge is in the realm of five elements and it is talked about as real or unreal so long as the knowledge 'I am' is there, it is a product of the knowledge 'I am'. A 'jnani' is that state from which the witnessing of the knowledge 'I am' takes place. In that 'jnani' state there is no touch of 'I amness' (it is a quality-less state) and it is not knowledge – knowledge means 'I amness'.

Not an individual but the knowledge 'I am' must go to its source. Out of the no-being comes the beingness. It comes as quietly as twilight; just a feel of 'I am' and then suddenly the space is there.

Reincarnation implies a reincarnating self. There is no such thing. The bundle of memories and hopes, called the "I", imagines itself existing everlastingly and creates time to accommodate its false eternity. To be, I need no past or future. All experience is born of imagination; I do not imagine, so no birth or death happens to me. Only those who think themselves born can think themselves re-born. All exists in awareness, and awareness neither dies nor is re-born. It is the changeless reality itself.

Remain focused on the 'I am' till it goes into oblivion, then the eternal is, the Absolute is, Parabrahman is.

Remember the knowledge 'I am' only and give up the rest, staying in the 'I am' you will realize that it is unreal.

Remember, nothing you perceive is your own.

What is really your own, you are not conscious of. You are nothing that you are conscious of.

Recorded religions are mere heaps of verbiage. Religions show their true face in action, in silent action. To know what a man believes, watch how he acts. For most of the people, service of their bodies and their minds is their religion. They may have religious ideas, but they do not act on them.

See everything as a dream, as a show, as a film.

Nothing stands in the way of your liberation and it can happen here and now but for your being more interested in other things. And you cannot fight with your interests. You must go with them, see through them and watch them reveal themselves as mere errors of judgment and appreciation.

Nothing you do will change you, for you need no change. You may change your mind or your body, but it is always something external to you that has changed, not yourself. Why bother at all to change? Realize once for all that neither your body nor your mind, nor even your consciousness is yourself and stand alone in your true nature beyond consciousness and unconsciousness. No effort can take you there, only the clarity of understanding.

Putting aside everything, stabilize in the 'I am'. As you continue with this practice, in the process you will transcend the 'I am'.

Nothings stops you from being a gnani here and now, except fear. You are afraid of being impersonal, of impersonal being. It is all quite simple. Turn away from your desires and fears and from the thoughts they create and you are at once in your natural state.

Reality is neither subjective nor objective, neither mind nor matter, neither time nor space. These divisions need somebody to whom to happen, a conscious separate center. But reality is all and nothing, the totality and the exclusion, the fullness and the emptiness, fully consistent, absolutely paradoxical. You cannot speak about it, you can only lose yourself in it. When you deny reality to anything, you come to a residue which cannot be denied.

Realization is but the opposite of ignorance. To take the world as real and one's self as unreal is ignorance, the cause of sorrow. To know the self as the only reality and all else as temporal and transient is freedom, peace and joy. It is all very simple. Instead of seeing things as imagined, learn to see them as they are. When you can see everything as it is, you will also see yourself as you are. It is like cleansing a mirror. The same mirror that shows you the world as it is, will also show you your own face. The thought "I am" is the polishing cloth. Use it.

Now coming to a very subtle situation, what is it in you that understands this knowledge 'you are' – or from your standpoint 'I am' without a name, title or word? Subside in that innermost center and witness the knowledge 'I am' and 'just be'; this is the bliss of being – the 'swarupananda'.

Refuse all thoughts except one: the thought "I am". The mind will rebel in the beginning, but with patience and perseverance it will yield and keep quiet. Once you are quiet, things will begin to happen spontaneously and quite naturally, without any interference on your part.

Refuse attention [to things], let things come and go. Desires and thoughts are also things. Disregard them. Since immemorial time, the dust of events was covering the clear mirror of your mind, so that only memories you could see. Brush off the dust before it has time to settle; this will lay bare the old layers until the true nature of your mind is discovered. It is all very simple and comparatively easy; be earnest and patient, that is all. Dispassion, detachment, freedom from desire and fear, from all self-concern, mere awareness, free from memory and expectation, this is the state of mind to which discovery can happen. After all, liberation is but the freedom to discover.

Now I know nothing, for all knowledge is in dream only and not valid. I know myself and I find no life nor death in me, only pure being, not being this or that, but just being.

Obviously, it is the sense of being present. In memory and anticipation, there is a clear feeling that it is a mental state under observation, while in the actual the feeling is primarily of being present and aware. Wherever you go, the sense of here and now you carry with you all the time. It means that you are independent of space and time, that space and time are in you, not you in them. It is your self-identification with the body, which, of course, is limited in space and time; that gives you the feeling of finiteness. In reality you are infinite and eternal.

Now what is it that we are concerned with? We are dealing with the physical form, which is made up of, and fed by, the five elements. In that form are operating the life force (the vital breath) and this consciousness that is, the knowledge 'I am' or the sense of being, the sense of existence. The latter is the 'sentience', which is the gift of the consciousness.

Of the unknowable only silence talks. The mind can talk only of what it knows. If you diligently investigate the knowable, it dissolves and only the unknowable remains. But with the first flicker of imagination and interest the unknowable is obscured and the known comes to the fore-front. The known, the changing, is what you live with; the unchangeable is of no use to you. It is only when you are satiated with the changeable and long for the unchangeable that you are ready for the turning round and stepping into what can be described, when seen from the level of the mind, as emptiness and darkness. For the mind craves for content and variety, while reality is, to the mind, contentless and invariable.

On my true, whole, homogenous state just a small ripple appeared, the news came, 'I am'. That news made all the difference, and I started knowing this; but now I have known my true state, so I understand my true state first, and then I understand that this ripple is coming and going on my true state. While in your case, you take interest in the ripple and don't take interest in your true state.

On the state of 'non-beingness', the beingness appeared together with manifestation, creating a feeling as if 'I am'; who that is, is not important, only 'I am' is important. The initial humming of the beingness as 'I am, I am' is the duality. But who accepts the duality? The 'non-beingness' accepts duality with the beingness. The Absolute 'non-being' state, by assuming the being state, becomes dual in manifestation.

Pose the question from the standpoint that you are only the knowledge 'I am'. The primary ignorance is about our 'I amness'; we have taken it as the Ultimate, which is ignorance. We presume that this consciousness is the eternal, the Ultimate, which is the mistake. This 'I am' principle is there provided the waking state and deep sleep are there. I am not the waking state, I am not the deep sleep – therefore I, the Absolute, am not that 'I am'. Leave aside this triad what are you? Understand clearly, when you keep aside the very instrument of questioning, where is the question?

Presently the feeling that you are is also memory. To sustain that memory of 'I am', all these raw materials are necessary. You are not that 'I am'. You are as the Absolute, prior to this 'I am'.

Primarily because of your identification with your body, you have polluted God. Because of your association with body, you have fear of death. There is no death only the vital breath departs and 'I am' disappears. Body is the sustenance of 'I amness' or Atman. I say, if you want to remember this visit, remember the knowledge 'I am', or remember the knowledge 'you are'.

Once it is understood that 'I am' is purely 'I am', formless and not that shackled body form – then no liberation is called for. To be stabilized in that beingness, which has no name and form, that itself is liberation.

Once the body and the sense of being('I am') goes what remains is the Original, which is unconditioned, without attributes, and without identity; that on which this temporary state of the consciousness and the three states and the three 'gunas' have come and gone. It is called 'Parabrahman', the Absolute.

Prior to birth there is no waking, sleeping or the beingness (the knowledge 'I am'), these three are born and are dependent on the food essence. When this essence becomes weak, the three states depart. Who is born or dies? In the absence of the three states, did you know God? Did you know that you existed?

Prior to the appearance of form in the womb, food stuffs take the form 'I am' and that appears in nine months. With birth the bodily functions begin, the child does not know that it is. As the child begins to identify, the sense of 'I amness' takes shape, only then the mother can teach the misleading headings like body name and so forth. Prior to the waking or sleep state is the Parabrahman. The state which gives you knowledge is Brahman.

Once a living being has heard and understood that deliverance is within his reach, he will never forget it, for it is the first message from within. It will take roots and grow and in due course take the blessed shape of the Guru.

Once the vital breath leaves the body and this 'I amness' ceases to exist, the 'I amness' will not know that 'It was'. The 'I amness' is not permanent and will forget its association with is body.

Pain and pleasure, good and bad, right and wrong: these are relative terms and must not be taken absolutely. They are limited and temporary.

Pain is physical, suffering is mental. Beyond the mind there is no suffering. Pain is essential for the survival of the body, but none compels you to suffer. Suffering is due entirely to clinging or resisting; it is a sign of our unwillingness to move on, to flow with life. As a sane life is free of pain, so is a saintly life free from suffering. A saint does not want things to be different from what they are; he knows that, considering all factors, they are unavoidable. He is friendly with the inevitable and, therefore, does not suffer. Pain he may know, but it does not shatter him. If he can, he does the needful to restore the lost balance, or he lets things take their course.

Once you are in it [true awareness], you will find that you love what you see, whatever may be its nature. This choiceless love is the touchstone of awareness. If it is not there, you are merely interested, for some personal reasons.

Paths and movements cannot transport you into Reality, because their function is to enmesh you within the dimensions of knowledge, while the Reality prevails prior to it. To apprehend this, you must stay put at the source of your creation, at the beginning of the knowledge 'I am'. So long as you do not achieve this, you will be entangled in the chains forged by your mind and get enmeshed in those of others.

Pleasure depends on things, happiness does not. As long as we believe that we need things to make us happy, we shall also believe that in their absence we must be miserable. Mind always shapes itself according to its beliefs. Hence the importance of convincing oneself that one need not be prodded into happiness; that, on the contrary, pleasure is a distraction and a nuisance, for it merely increases the false conviction that one needs to have and do things to be happy, when in reality it is just the opposite. But why talk of happiness at all? You do not think of happiness except when you are unhappy. A man who says "Now I am happy" is between two sorrows, past and future. This happiness is mere excitement caused by relief from pain. Real happiness is utterly unselfconscious. It is best expressed negatively as: "there is nothing wrong with me, I have nothing to worry about".

Once you realize that all happens by itself (call it destiny, or the will of God, or mere accident), you remain as witness only, understanding and enjoying, but not perturbed. You are responsible only for what you can change. All you can change is only your attitude. There lies your responsibility.

Once you realize that the person is merely a shadow of the reality, but not reality itself, you cease to fret and worry. You agree to be guided from within and life becomes a journey into the unknown.

Once you realize that the road is the goal and that you are always on the road, not to reach a goal, but to enjoy its beauty and its wisdom, life ceases to be a task and becomes natural and simple, in itself an ecstasy.

Once you reject what you are not, whatever finally remains, the leftover, is yourself – your true nature. Presently, whatever you know is 'I am', this 'I am' is the product of the five elements. Out of the elements comes the food body and because of the food body, that 'I amness' is sustained. And you are also not that 'I am'. 'I am' is the taste, the fragrance of this food body. The ultimate 'you' has no fragrance, no taste, no touch of 'I amness'.

Once you subside into the consciousness, the factual state of Reality shall be revealed to you with the knowledge that will emanate out of you intuitively, like spring water. This will enable you to discern not what is real and unreal, but, most importantly, to realize what 'I am'. And who could be that one? Surely not an individual who is trapped in the mind-shell, but that one is the knowledge 'I am' – the consciousness.

Only the 'I am' is certain, it's impersonal, all knowledge stems from it, it's the root, hold on to it and let all else go.

Only your sense 'I am', though in the world, is not of the world. By no effort of logic you can change the 'I am' into 'I am not'. In the very denial of your being you assert it. Once you realize that the world is your own projection, you are free of it. You need not free yourself of a world that does not exist, except in your imagination.

Originally, I am untainted – uncovered by anything, without stigma – since nobody existed prior to me. Nor do I entertain any concepts about somebody existing, before me. Everything is in the form of the manifested world, after the appearance of the knowledge 'I am' with the body. Together with the body and the indwelling 'I amness' everything is. Prior to the appearance of this body and the knowledge 'I am', what was there?

Out of the nothingness, the 'I am' or beingness has come, there is no individual, the knowledge 'I am'- not the individual – has to go back to its source.

One cannot see rays of light, as such; they reflect only when they encounter another object. Similarly 'I amness' is the interruption because of these five elements and three 'gunas'. That is why the feeling 'I am' is felt; but without the feeling of 'I am', still you are.

The witness cannot 'be' in the absence of the knowledge 'I am'. Who are you seeing if you are not aware of the 'I am'? You have covered everything with this 'I am' knowledge. The five elemental world is only the creation of this 'I amness'.

One has to understand that the search for reality, God, Guru and the search for the self are the same, when one is found all are found. When 'I am' and 'God is' become in your mind indistinguishable, then something will happen and you will know without a trace of doubt that God is because you are, you are because God is. The two are one.

The witness is both unreal and real. The last remnant of the illusion, the first touch of the real. To say: I am only the witness is both false and true, false because of the 'I am', true because of the witness. It is better to say: 'there is witnessing'. The moment you say 'I am', the entire universe comes into being along with its creator.

One is the Absolute, two is consciousness, and three is space. Where there was no knowledge 'I am' that is number one, later on there is the sense 'I am' that is number two, and then there is space – number three.

One who has realized the knowledge 'I am', which means transcending it as well, for him there is no birth or death nor any karma.

The witness is merely a point in awareness. It has no name and form. It is like the reflection of the sun in a drop of dew. The drop of dew has name and form, but the little point of light is caused by the sun.

The knowledge 'I am' is nothing. That knowledge is like a guest; it comes and goes. You have come here; you are very clever. Now what did happen? All the knowledge, which you had collected elsewhere and brought here, is rendered useless and redundant. So long as beingness is there, all worldly activities will go on. But you now realize that 'You' are neither the activities in the beingness nor the beingness. 'You' as the Absolute, are none of these.

One who is completely rid of coming and going, and finally, one who is completely rid of one's very own concept that 'I am', is completely liberated.

Only that individual who has lost his individuality has merged with the 'Parabrahman'. So the individuality must go. The entire world moves on the basis of one concept, and that is 'I am' – the fundamental concept of one's individuality.

The knowledge 'I am' is the film, the destiny. Finally what is our destiny? It is that birth chemical, that film in which everything is recorded and everything is happening. Where are 'you' in this?

The knowledge 'I am' is the first ignorance and whatever knowledge you acquire with it is ignorance. Go back to the source of your ignorance.

The knowledge 'I am' is the product of interaction within the five elemental state, You are not that! You as the Absolute, are not the knowledge 'I am'.

The knowledge 'I am' is the same, whether it is an insect, worm, human being or an avatar (being of the highest order); the basic consciousness is the same in all of these.

The knowledge 'I am' is the soul of the entire world. The witness of the knowledge 'I am' is prior to the knowledge 'I am'. Try to understand yourself as you are, do not add any qualifications.

Written Words of Nisargadatta

Atmajnana and Paramatmayoga, "Self-Knowledge and Self-Realization"

(Editor's Note) I conclude this work with the only known published book Nisargadatta Maharaj had written himself in 1963. Although the content is leans far more toward the devotional than what we find in his talks in the 70s and early 80s, the great master's perfume is nonetheless all over it.

1. DIVINE VISION AND THE DEVOTEE

Divine vision means acquaintance with, and crystalline understanding of, the universal energy. God and the devotee are one, in his very nature the devotee is identical with God. So long as one has not realized God, one does not know what justice and injustice are, but with realization the devotee comes to know the distinction between justice and injustice, the essential and the contingent, the eternal and the evanescent, and this leads to his emancipation.

The divine vision eliminates individuality; the manifest is clearly distinguished from the unmanifest. When the sense of individuality is replaced by that of impersonal consciousness the devotee knows that he is pure consciousness. Manifestation is pure consciousness manifesting itself in all the different names and forms; the spiritually enlightened take part in it sportively, knowing that it is only the play of universal consciousness.

The name and form of the spiritually enlightened Saint experiences the pangs and sorrows of life, but not their sting. He is neither moved nor perturbed by the pleasures and pains, nor the profits and losses of the world. He is thus in a position to direct others. His behavior is guided exclusively by the sense of justice.

The temporal life must continue, with all its complex interactions, but the Saint is ever aware that it is only the pure consciousness that is expressing itself in different names and forms, and it continues to do so, in ever new forms. To him, the unbearable events of the world are just a tame and harmless affair; he remains unmoved in world-shaking events.

At first people, through pride, simply ignore him, but their subsequent experiences draw them toward him. God, as justice incarnate, has neither relations nor belongings of His own; peace and happiness are, as it were, His only treasure. The formless, divine consciousness cannot have anything as its own interest.

This is the temporal outline of the Bhakta.

2. THE SOUL, THE WORLD, BRAHMAN AND SELF REALIZATION

The consciousness of one's own being, of the world, and of its supporting primal force are experienced all at once. Awareness of one's own being does not mean here the physical consciousness of oneself as an individual, but implies the mystery of existence. Prior to this, in the ignorance of one's own being, there is no experience of Brahman as being there. But the moment one is aware of being, he is directly aware of the world and Brahman, too.

At the stage prior to this cosmic awareness, the self and its experiences are limited to the worldly life. This worldly life starts with birth and ends in death. To become aware of our self, the world and God all of a sudden is a great mystery indeed. It is an unexpected gain; it is an absorbing and a mysterious event, extremely significant and great, but it brings with it the responsibility of Self-preservation, sustenance and Self development as well, and no one can avoid it.

One who leads his life without ever wondering about who or what he is accepts the traditional genealogical history as his own and follows the customary religious and other activities according to tradition. He leads his life with the firm conviction that the world was there prior to his existence, and that it is real; because of this conviction he behaves as he does, gathering possessions and treasures for himself, even knowing that at the time of death he will never see them again. Knowing that none of this will even be remembered after death, still his greed and avarice operate unabated until death.

3. SELF KNOWLEDGE AND SELF REALIZATION

When we concentrate our attention on the origin of thought, the thought process itself comes to an end; there is a hiatus, which is pleasant, and again the process starts. Turning from the external world and enjoying the objectless bliss, the mind feels that the world of objects is not for it. Prior to this experience the unsatiating sense enjoyments constantly challenged the mind to satisfy them, but from the inward turn onwards its interest in them begins to fade. Once the internal bliss is enjoyed, the external happiness loses its charm. One who has tasted the inward bliss is naturally loving and free from envy, contented and happy with others' prosperity, friendly and innocent and free from deceit. He is full of the mystery and wonder of the bliss. One who has realized the Self can never inflict pain on other.

4. LIFE DIVINE AND THE SUPREME SELF

With heartfelt love and devotion, the devotee propitiates God; and when he is blessed with His vision and grace, he feels ever happy in His presence. The constant presence establishes a virtual identity between the two. While seeking the presence of the Supreme Soul, the Bhakta renounces all associations in his life, from the meanest to the best, and having purged his being of all associations, he automatically wins the association with the Supreme Self. One who has attained to the position of unstinted emancipation can never be disliked by others, for the people themselves are the very Self-luminous soul, though ignorant of the fact.

In this world of immense variety, different beings are suffering from different kinds of ailments, and yet they are not prepared to give up the physical frame, even when wailing under physical and mental pain. If this be so, then men will not be so short-sighted as to avoid their savior, the enlightened soul.

That overflowing reservoir of bliss, the beatific soul, does confer only bliss on the people by his loving light. Even the atmosphere around him heartens the suffering souls. He is like the waters of a lake that gives nourishment to the plants and trees around the brink and the grass and fields nearby. The Saint gives joy and sustaining energy to the people around him.

5. THE ASPIRANT AND SPIRITUAL THOUGHT

Spiritual thought is of the Highest. This seeking of the Highest is called the "first half" by the Saints. A proper understanding of this results in the vision of God, and eventually matures into the certainty of the true nature of the Self in the "latter half".

One who takes to the path of the spirit starts with contemplation and propitiation. It is here, for the first time, that he finds some joy in prayer and worship. At this preliminary stage he gets the company of co-aspirants. Reading of the lives and works of past incarnations of God, of Rishis, of Saints and Sages, singing the glories of the Name, visiting temples, and a constant meditation on these result in the photic and phonic experiences of the mystic life; his desires are satisfied to an extent now. Thinking that he has had the vision of God, he intensifies his efforts of fondly remembering the name of God and His worship. In this state of the mind, the Bhakta quite frequently has a glimpse of his cherished deity, which he takes to be the divine vision and is satisfied with it. At this juncture, he is sure to come into contact with a Saint.

The Saint, and now his preceptor, makes it plain to him that what he has had is not the real vision, which is beyond the said experiences, and is only to be had through Self Realization. At this point, the aspirant reaches the stage of the meditator. In the beginning, the Sadhaka is instructed into the secrets of his own person, and of the indwelling spirit; the meaning and nature of prana, the various plexuses, and the nature and arousal of the Kundalini, and the nature of the Self. Later on, he comes to know of the origin of the five elements, their activity, radiation, and merits and defects. Meanwhile his mind undergoes the process of purification and acquires composure, and this the Sadhaka experiences through the deep-laid subtle center of the Indweller; he also knows how and why it is there, only that the deiform element is kindled. This knowledge transforms him into the pure, eternal, and spiritual form of a SadGuru who is now in a position to initiate others into the secrets of the spirit. The stage of Sadhakahood ends here.

As the great Saint Tukarama said, the aspirant must put in ceaseless efforts in the pursuit of spiritual life. Thoughts must be utilized for Self-Knowledge. He must be alert and watchful in ascertaining the nature of this "I" that is involved in the affairs of pleasure and pain arising out of sense experience.

We must know the nature of the active principle lest its activities be led astray. We should not waste our energies in useless pursuits, but should use those energies in the pursuit of the Self and achieve identity with God. Spiritual life is so great, so deep, so immense, that energy pales into insignificance before it, yet this energy tries to understand it again and again. Those who try to understand it with the help of the intellect are lost to it.

Rare is the one who, having concentrated on the source atom of the cosmic energy, enjoys the bliss of spiritual contemplation. But there are scores of those who take themselves to be spiritually inspired and perfect beings. They expect the common herd to honor and respect their every word. The ignorant people rush towards them for spiritual succor and do their bidding. In fact, the pseudo-Saints are caught in a snare of greed, hence what the people get in return is not the blessings of satisfaction, but ashes.

The self-styled man of God, speaking ad nauseum about spiritual matters, thinks himself to be perfect, but others are not so sure. As regards a Saint, on the other hand, men are on the lookout for ways to serve him more and more, but as the ever contented soul, steeped in beatitude, desires nothing, they are left to serve in their own way, which they do with enthusiasm, and they never feel the pressure.

Greatness is always humble, loving, silent and satisfied. Happiness, tolerance, forbearance, composure and other allied qualities must be known by everyone; just as one experiences bodily states such as hunger, thirst, etc., one. must, with equal ease, experience in oneself the characteristics connoted by the word "Saint". As we know for certain that we need no more sleep, no more food, at a given moment, so too we can be sure of the above characteristics from direct experience. One can then recognize their presence in others with the same ease. This is the test and experience of a tried spiritual leader.

6. THE MYSTIC

The blissful mystic clearly sees the difference between his characteristics before and after realization. All that is transient has an origin in time and is subject to change and destruction, while he is free from change and can never perish. The unchanging one views the ever changing world as a game.

All the characteristics of the Saint naturally spring from his experience. As there are no desires left in him, nothing in the world of sense can ever tempt him, he lives in the fearless majesty of Self-realization. He is moved to pity by the unsuccessful struggle of those tied down to bodily identity and their striving for the satisfaction of their petty interests. Even the great events of the world are just surface lines to him; the number of these lines that appear and disappear is infinite.

Individuals are only the faint streaks of these lines, and only as such lines are they recognized. When the streaks vanish there remains nothing to recognize as individuals.

The interval between the moment of emergence and the disappearance of a line is what is called life. The wiped out line can never be seen again.

The Saint who has direct experience of all this is always happy and free from desire. He is convinced that the greatest of the sense experiences is only a momentary affair, impermanence is the very essence of these experiences; hence pain and sorrow, greed and temptation, fear and anxiety can never touch him.

7. THE LILA OF GOD

Sport or play is natural to God, our experiences are known as the Lila (play) of God. Without any prior intimation, we suddenly have a taste of our own being; excepting this one instance of the taste, we have no knowledge of the nature of the Self. But then, even this bit of experience is hidden away from us. We are forced into a series of activities and experiences: that I am a homosapien, I am a body, my name is such and such, this is my religion, my duty, etc. One action follows another, and there is no rest from them, no escape, we have to see them through. This goes on inevitably, until perchance, it loses all its charm, and we seek the spiritual treasure.

If the purpose of all this be inquired into, we get different accounts from different people. Some claim it is because of the actions of millions of previous lives – but nobody has the direct experience of these past lives; it is obvious that this is fiction.

Dazzled by the ingenious inventions and discoveries of the scientists, some base their interpretation on empirical facts and offer them as explanations, but the suddenly experienced taste of our own being cannot be interpreted in this way. When the world is called by the word Maya or illusion, it is condemned to be mean; when the same thing is called by the words "play of God", it becomes great! In reality the facts are what they are. Who is the recipient of the high designation – who confirms the uselessness for the condemnation – who is He – what name should we give Him after first-hand experience?

That we have experiences is a fact; others tell us about their experiences, we receive information concerning relations, and instruction in the performance of activities, and we organize our behavior accordingly. Someone from these guides initiates us into what is said to be the core of the indwelling Spirit, but that too turns out to be a transient affair. For the acquaintance secured thus does not possess the experiential core of the taste, and the initiator himself proves to be part and parcel of that bit; thus both he and his knowledge are lost to us. Now we are free to go our own way, but for want of the necessary taste, this self-help is equally helpless. We are where we were.

What is it that we call the Lila of God? How are we related to this sporting God whom we saw, talked to, had friendship with, and intense love for. In spite of all this closeness and fondness, what is our relation to Him? All the previous experiences with their peculiarities have vanished. The Lila of God disappears along with the pseudo experience with the advent of the present experience.

8. THE SPIRITUAL ASPIRANT, THE FIRST MOMENT OF BLISS AND ITS CONTINUOUS GROWTH

The ever-awaited first moment was the moment when I was convinced that I was not an individual at all. The idea of my individuality had set me burning so far. The scalding pain was beyond my capacity to endure; but there is not even a trace of it now, I am no more an individual. There is nothing to limit my being now. The ever present anxiety and the gloom have vanished and now I am all beatitude, pure knowledge, pure consciousness.

The tumors of innumerable desires and passion were simply unbearable, but fortunately for me, I got hold of the hymn "Hail, Preceptor", and on its constant recitation, all the tumors of passions withered away as with a magic spell!

I am ever free now. I am all bliss, sans spite, sans fear. This beatific conscious form of mine now knows no bounds. I belong to all and everyone is mine. The "all" are but my own individuations, and these together go to make up my beatific being. There is nothing like good or bad, profit or loss, high or low, mine or not mine for me. Nobody opposes me and I oppose none for there is none other than myself. Bliss reclines on the bed of bliss. The repose itself has turned into bliss.

There is nothing that I ought or ought not to do, but my activity goes on everywhere, every minute. Love and anger are divided equally among all, as are work and recreation. My characteristics of immensity and majesty, my pure energy, and my all, having attained to the golden core, repose in bliss as the atom of atoms. My pure consciousness shines forth in majestic splendor.

Why and how the consciousness became self-conscious is obvious now. The experience of the world is no more of the world as such, but is the blossoming forth of the selfsame conscious principle, God, and what is it? It is pure, primal knowledge, conscious form, the primordial "I" consciousness that is capable of assuming any form it desires. It is designated as God. The world as the divine expression is not for any profit or loss; it is the pure, simple, natural flow of beatific consciousness. There are no distinctions of God and devotee, nor Brahman and Maya. He that meditated on the bliss and peace is himself the ocean of peace and bliss. Glory to the eternal truth, Sad-Guru, the Supreme Self.

9. DEVOTEE AND THE BLESSINGS OF GOD

The Bhakta pours out his devotion, molds his behavior in every respect in accordance with the will of God. In turn, he finds that God is pleased with him, and this, his conviction, takes him nearer to God and his love and friendship with Him grow richer and richer. The process of surrendering to the will of God in every respect results in His blessings.

One who is blessed by God is a blissful soul. Being at peace with himself, he looks at the objects of enjoyment with perfect indifference. He is content with whatever he has and is glad to see others happy. If a person believes that he is blessed by God and is still unhappy, it is better if he give up this delusion and strive for the coveted Grace with sincerity and honesty.

Divine plenitude and favor is not judged by the objects of sense, but by the internal contentment. This verily is the blessing of God.

10. THE UNITIVE LIFE

Him have I seen now whom I so earnestly desired to see, I met myself. The meeting requires an extremely difficult and elaborate preparation.

I pined to see the most beloved one. It was impossible to do without it, I was sure to die if I were not to do it. Even with the innermost sincerity of my whole being I was not able to get at it, and the situation was unbearable. Yet with love and determination, eagerness and courage, I started on my journey. I had to get through different stages and places in the undertaking.

Being quite deft, it would not allow me cognition, at first. But lo, I saw it today, I was sure, but the very next moment I felt perhaps it was not it. Whenever I saw it I was intent on observing it keenly, but not knowing its nature with certitude, could not decide either way. I could not be sure that it was my Beloved, the center of my being. Being an adept in the art of make-up, it dodged me with a quick change of form ere I could arrive at a conclusion. These were the visions of various Incarnations of Rishis and Saints, internal visions in the process of Dhyana and Dharana, and external ones of the waking state eventual to the siddhis, such as the power of prophecy, clairvoyance, clairaudience, and the power to cure normally incurable diseases, etc. Some were eager to serve me, to have faith in me and to honor me, and this led me to believe that I had seen it for certain; it is here its skill in make-up lies. It is so deft in the art of changing the form, quality and knowledge, that the intellect does not know where it stands, let alone the penetration through its nature. But, what is this miracle? Wonder of wonders! The flash, curiously glistening, majestic splendor! But where is it? It disappeared in a flicker before I could apprehend it. No, nothing could be known about what happened to me or to the lightning. I could not say whether the extremely swift flash and the means of my reconnaissance were one and the same or different. In the glow of the flashing miracle the whole of the cosmic array is experienced directly. The contact is immensely interesting. The flash experience makes one feel it should be as spicy forever; this is the characteristic feeling of the cosmic experience. But in the very attempt to arrest the glowing flash for a basic understanding, one loses it.

It is extremely difficult to get at the root of the cosmic energy, that perfect adept in assuming an infinite variety of forms. The consciousness to be apprehended and the power of concentration are one and the same. Being polymorphous by nature, it cannot be pinned down to any definite form or name or place, as for instance, the internal experiences of the Dhyana yogin. In the first instance, the attention of the meditator is silence in excelsis, this is transformed into light, the light assumes the form of space, the space in turn changes into movement. This is transmitted into air, and the air into fire, the fire changes into water, and the water into earth. Lastly, the earth evolves into the world of organic and inorganic things. The water from the rain takes the form of the juices in the grains and vegetables, which essences supply nourishment and energy. This energy takes the form of knowledge, courage, valor, cunning, etc. The limbless process goes on. Neither form, name, nor quality is enduring. Nothing is permanent or determinate.

The felt experience of the spiritually enlightened is difficult to negotiate with. This may mean either that it is beyond our capacity to get at, or it is beyond reach; yet one must go on with concentration. The identity of the "I" as the miracle in the process of the dazzling glitter, and the "ego" of the empirical consciousness prior to the experience, must be firmly established in Dhyana Yoga (meditation). Is the spiritually saturated soul the same as the experience or is it even beyond that? There is no duality to the experience one has in the process of Dhyana Yoga. At the enlightened stage even the sense organs are involved in the meditation of the spiritual adept, for the sense organs and the five elements are one and the same at the core. The material elements, subtle matter and consciousness, the three qualities, Satva, Rajas and Tamas, and the three sources of knowledge, perception, inference and testimony were seen, are being seen, and lo! They are not there.

The characteristics of origination, sustenance and destruction come under Dhyana Yoga itself. The activity of Prakriti in all its forms, manifest and unmanifest, and the consciousness of Purusha are also included in it. In the Dhyana Yoga process the eight chakras are activated simultaneously and are experienced as such. All these, in a single, unitive experience, I constitute the contemplation. Meditation, consciousness, experience, are all but a single unity.

Dhyana Yoga is the supreme activity of life. Concentration is the central thing in experience.

The transformation of Dhyana Yoga into Mama [sic] Yoga is a difficult process. In the consummation of this process alone is the Atman cognized with certitude. As long as Dhyana Yoga is not completely transformed into Jnana Yoga, so long there is no Self knowledge. The test of Dhyana is knowledge, then follows the duality of knowledge and the Atman. In the experiential knowledge, there is a race between knowledge as Self and Self as Self. But in deep samadhi there is an understanding between contemplation and the Self. This results in the realization of bliss. The bliss is transformed into supreme beatitude and the self is absorbed in the supreme Spirit. Knowledge to itself, contemplation into itself, the primal Maya, God, the Absolute state and the original throb are all a single whole of Self-experience. The ever cherished and desired Being is realized here.

Prior to this, in the process of the attainment of the siddhis incidental to Dhyana Yoga, there ooze forth experiences in the form of arts, love, and memories of past lives in different regions such as Patala, Swarga and Kailas. In some cases one has a taste of different siddhis and Avatars and of a series of meetings with others in different regions. There are experiences of being the Brahma of Satya region, Shiva of Kailas, and Vishnu of Vaikunth from time immemorial. Again, there are different phases of the yogin's feelings, the best and the worst, and the endless panoramas, not pleasant nor enduring; and the inevitable adjuncts of Dhyana Yoga must go on until it is transformed into Jnana Yoga; i.e., the transition from the Samprajuata (silent mind in meditation) to the Asamprajuata (altered state of consciousness, silent and alert mind) state of samadhi. Until then there is no Self-realization. But, on the other hand, if in the process of this transition the nature of this phase of Dhyana Yoga be known, Self-realization is automatic.

All the experiences and visions arising out of Dhyana Yoga are transitory. In the contemplation, there is an infinite variety of phases and forms, and none of them is lasting. Whatever is taken to be helpful and great and determinate vanishes in an instant and a new form takes its place to yield place to the next. That knowledge from which all the varieties issue forth in experiences, such as earth, water, fire, air, ether, and their various specifications, is itself unstable. Starting from meditation, the contemplating soul, having experienced a taste of previous lives, is further transformed into the primal Maya, primordial energy, and Godhead, and even into the characteristics of the supreme Self by the power of meditation, and all this for a trice, and it disappears. It is here that it is called Kala, the final liquidation of individuality. It is here that the separation from itself is compensated for, and finds itself with spiritual certitude, never to be lost again. The imperishable, indissoluble, eternal Paramatman shines forth with perfection beyond the reach of empirical experience.

11. KNOW WHAT ?

The continuous process of getting to know the environment goes on from the birth of the "I" consciousness. Though the "I" consciousness is automatic, hence effortless, one has to learn to do various things; one also must learn about one's own person and its care. Some things are mastered of necessity, and of one's liking; others which are not essential must also be learnt.

In the process of conscious learning, over and above the world of things, we are told we must also learn of the things beyond the world; but before trying to know the things beyond, we must know the controller and support of the universe called God, so that other things may be known with His help.

Who is God and how is He to be propitiated? We are told that this is to be achieved by forming friendship with saintly persons and by regularly and devoutly carrying out their instructions; but then, we are told, it is a matter of rare good fortune that one comes across such a saintly soul, and when one comes across such a person, by rare good fortune, the saintly soul tells us, "You yourself are God. Think of Him alone, meditate on

His being. Do not engage yourself in thinking of anybody else."

For a while I used to deal with various matters and perform activities such as knowing and learning with the idea that I was a human being, born of the "I" consciousness; next I started meditating on myself as God in order to know myself. Now I know that I am the knower of whatever I remember, perceive, or feel; hence, ignoring all that is remembered, perceived, or felt, I contemplate on the nature of the knower.

I am sitting in a secluded place where none can see me, with my eyes half closed.

Whatever I remember, perceive, feel or experience comes into being from within myself. My meditation is my torch and what I see is its light, all that I see and remember is just the light of my meditation.

Now I do not feel the necessity to meditate anymore, for the nature of meditation is such that it is spontaneous. In its process, it gives rise to innumerable forms and names and qualities and what have I got to do with it all?

Now I am convinced beyond doubt that this meditation of mine is born of God; and the world of things is the product of my meditation only. The cyclic process of origination, sustenance and destruction is the very core of the world's being. However more I may try to know, the same process must repeat. My inquisitiveness has come to an end.

12. SPIRITUAL BLISS

The spiritual aspirant is absorbed in his spiritual experiments and experiences, and the journey continues. One already has the experience of the world through his senses, hence he tries, as far as possible, to depend only on himself, he tries to gauge the extent to which he can go with the minimum of help from others and eschews the use of many things in the world. In due course, the aspirant is sure to win peace; nothing is wanting, he has enough and to spare. He is satisfied and his behavior reveals it. He expects nothing from those with whom he deals. Is expecting material returns from others any different from begging? If it is true that he has attained to happiness beyond the reach of ordinary mortals, why should he expect a beggarly share from material gains? If he has in his possession the blissful spring of eternal life, why should he ask a price from his dealings with others? It is impossible that one who has realized his Self should rely on others; on the contrary, he feeds others on spiritual food with absolute ease.

As the happiness of the people increases, they begin to love him with greater sincerity, they know his importance in their lives. Just as they acquire and store food, so too they take care of one who has attained the position of eternal peace, identity with the universal spirit, perfection. Yet some people get to know some occult processes from great Saints and practice them, enabling them to acquire certain occult powers and they are misled into thinking they have what they have been striving for, and style themselves as Raja yogins, and engage in the avid pursuit of material pleasures; but one who has tasted the pure bliss of eternal life in Brahman is forever satisfied, the perfect soul does not desire worldly honors.

It is impossible that the spiritually perfect soul should ever desire to be called the preceptor or to make others bow down before him or to expect all to honor his word in every respect. One who gets the highest kind of happiness from his life source has no interest in material happiness. That is spiritual happiness which makes everyone happy. These are the external qualities characterizing the enlightened satyagrahin (seeker of truth).

13. THE TENDER HEART OF THE SAINT

The heart of a mother is full of tenderness, but it is limited to her child only; but the heart of the Saint is all inclusive, it knows the how and whence of the origin of each one and the vicissitudes they have to go through.

The Saint is full of spiritual knowledge and pacific repose, there is nothing wanting. He practices his sadhana in such a way as not to be discovered by others; he has no use for the external marks of saintliness, he dresses in keeping with the time and climate.

Being in touch with the atom, the first cause of the universe, he knows its nature quite well. Blossoming forth is the very nature of the core of this atom, hence changes and differentiation are bound to be there. Knowing this well, the Saint is neither elated by pleasing events nor depressed by the opposite ones.

He has gauged the depth of the knowledge of the common man. He knows its nature from beginning to end. He knows the how and the why of the mentality, also the worthlessness of its achievements and failures. The needs of the body prompt the creature to acquire means of sustenance, but the greed for these makes the creature pursue them to the point of uselessness, and all of this without the least idea of what awaits the life in future. What the creature deems essential and strives to acquire, the Saint knows to be sheer trash.

The Saint is never a victim of passions. Life is a mixture of passions and emotions; Atman, the origin of passions and emotions, is the very core of the Saint's vision, the nature of which he is thoroughly acquainted. He knows its activities and varieties of manifestation, as well as their consequences. The life principle is the principle of feelings, passions, emotions. Desires and passions engendered in this principle are just emotive experiences, they have nothing of substance in them; yet the poor creature thinks them to be of great significance in his life, embraces the basically worthless desires, indulges in sense enjoyment, and runs after them helplessly.

The mother, with sincerity but in ignorance, feeds the roots of misery, while the Saint, with the same intensity, weeds them out. The Saint knows what the welfare of the people lies in much better than does the mother of her child. That is why the heart of the Saint is said to be kind.

14. DEVOTION TO BALAKRISHNA AND HIS CARE

During the process of Bhakta, Bhajan, and renunciation, the experience of the immensity of God is on the increase, but as the vision becomes more frequent, it gets narrower day by day. Here vision and knowledge are identical. In whatever name and form God is propitiated, that name and form he presents himself in. The various forms and names are woven into prayers and hymns and are sung by the common man.

The devotee by his firm determination, and God by his fascination for devotion, are attracted to each other and the moment they come face to face they merge; the devotee loses his phenomenal consciousness automatically, and when it returns he finds that he has lost his identity, lost into that of God and can never be separated again; God everywhere and no separate identity.

The creator, enjoyer, and destroyer of all names and forms, the controller of all powers, is revealed now; this is God, the Self, Self-luminous, Self-inspired, and Selfconscient. Here is where the primal gunas originate. Though atomic in character, he has in him the absolute power to do what he wills, in accordance with the emotive character of the gunas, and to take any form. This is the atomic center, atomic energy, the first and final cause of the universe.

The God of Gods, the soul of the movable and immovable, the all-pervasive, qualified Brahman, the beloved of the Bhaktas, the ocean of love and devotion is born here. This is

Adinarayana, residing in the hearts of the devotees; the Saints call him Balakrishna (Baby Krishna), for in the beginning he is seen to be the atom of atoms. By nature, he is innocence incarnate. He is easily moved by emotions and becomes many (immense), in accordance with the direction taken by the emotions. The nature of the expansion is determined by the excess of one or another of the three gunas. He manifests himself through each of the three gunas at different times in a non-partisan spirit. As the Saints are closely acquainted with him, they know what guna he would induce at any given moment and what the consequences would be, and hence they dissuade him from the excess of his nature. Excess of growth in any guna is dangerous. Satva guna is absolutely good, yet even that is harmful when hypertrophied; Rajas is restless and overbearing, while Tamas is blind and arrogant. Knowing this well, the wise man keeps his soul away from the effects of the gunas, hence the energy of the soul remains undiminished and develops in the right direction.

Satisfying various desires increases the taste for them, and the thirst for enjoyment slowly decreases the power of the soul in imperceptible degrees, but when, setting aside the temptation of the gunas, the devotee finds his pure soul, he fondly takes to its rearing with love and sincerity; only when the devotion is successful is the Atman realized. He is seen as a child at the dawn of victory, hence he is called the child of victory.

The Bhakta is alert not to allow it to be polluted by the craving for sensuous pleasures; the firmer it is in its nature, the greater becomes the power and strength of the soul, hence the Saints do not allow it to lose its steadiness. The crux of rearing it lies in keeping it firm, undeflected by the presence of the gunas. If the spiritual gain of the soul be eclipsed by sensuous desires, it is shaken to its very roots. It is difficult to keep the gunas at rest, that is why the Saints advise stabilizing in Self-knowledge.

15. SELF KNOWLEDGE AND SELF REALIZATION

Those who have realized and stabilized in Self-knowledge are those whose glory is sung from time immemorial; it is their names that form the basis of divine meditation. Sri Krishna, Sri Vishnu, and Sri Rama are some of the innumerable names given to God; originally, these were the names given to the human form, but they became Self-realized and came to know the root cause of all experience. Those who came to possess this knowledge of the Self and kept it pure and secure are known to be Gods and Saints, while those who utilized it for the sake of sense enjoyment are called devils and Ravanas. The highest and rarest gain is difficult of achievement, but, if achieved, it is superlatively beneficent, and if not properly cared for, is equally harmful. One who does not get excited by the possession of spiritual knowledge of the root cause can, with love and devotion, cultivate and brighten it. Devotion and prayer and renunciation are firmly established in him, he is always free from desires, and wherever he is the aura of peace and happiness is about him; the auriole shown about the heads of great Saints is a pictorial representation of this fact. Whoever approaches him gets an unsolicited touch of the divine bliss. The Saint never acts as an individual, all his actions are the expression of the divine Lila.

16. SPIRITUAL KNOWLEDGE AND THE PACIFICATION OF THE DESIRE TO KNOW

This universe came into being through the activity of the primal atomic (atmic) consciousness. There was nothing, not even a trace of appearance before self-consciousness, and in this state there came into being the consciousness of one's own existence, the awareness of one's own being. In fact, there was no time, nor space, nor cause. The awareness has no cause for it, hence it is futile to name one. There was no time, hence it cannot be dated. There was no space, hence its location is meaningless; yet the atomic consciousness was felt as such and nothing more – why so? For there was nothing over and above it to be aware of! The awareness only of being was there. How long this state lasted, there are no means to ascertain; but the great miracle is that the self-consciousness was there; with it was the cosmic will, followed by its realization. The atomic consciousness, on account of its will and its instant realization, became many and pervasive. Although apparently many, it is all one in essence.

When the atomic consciousness became many and pervasive on account of its will and its instantaneous realization, the energy of the single atom diversified itself into many centers, each with its own peculiarity and will; hence the conflict. At any given moment, the innumerable centers express their will in a variety of ways; generally, the willing atom does not know the "whither" and "what" of its will, but the effect is bound to be there. The tangible result of the wills of the willing atoms is to be witnessed at the moment of cosmic destruction, when the whole universe is reduced to ashes. The loving wills are not canceled altogether; the great moments of happiness in the world are the result of these wills. The characteristic of the individual energy to will is always operative. It is its essence and it owes it to the primordial energy.

The primal energy that scintillated first is one and homogeneous, but appears to be heterogeneous due to ignorance.

The quivering atomic energy is designated as the Great Principle by the Vedantas: the essential characteristic of the Principle is consciousness. The felt awareness expands itself into ether, the expanse of the ether is the space. With a single quality this Great Principle became time, space and cause. Next came the three gunas and the five elements. The speed was simply immeasurable.

The original scintillation moved in space and that was the air, the air gathered momentum and fire came into existence. The throbbing of the fire increased and became cold and that was water; the water cooled even more and that was earth. All the characteristics of the previous forms are crystallized in the earth and vibrate there; in virtue of this peculiarity there came into being innumerable varieties of living beings and vegetation, and the original quiver pulsates in and through their vital sap. The original will pervades the whole range of moving and immovable things and is constantly active there.

The scintillating characteristic prior to ether is filling every electron and proton and is constantly increasing in strength. As long as the quiver in the atoms is operative, so long the constituents must be in motion. The original will pervades the whole range of moving and immovable beings and is constantly active there.

The original consciousness sees nothing except itself. It has no organs, yet it is in action with innumerable Spiritual Knowledge and the Pacification of the Desire to Know

It is never polluted. The various conscious centers hedged by the limiting adjuncts only think they are different from the original source, but there is only one being, one spirit, one quality; formless, timeless, non-spatial, the one, pure consciousness. There is no scope for difference or distinction. The creature, deluded by the narrow interests of "I" and "mine", suffers pain for nothing, it is limited only to itself. Everything takes place at the proper moment, in accordance with the law that binds all, and everything materializes at the proper moment. When Ravana becomes unbearable Rama is there to give relief. When Kamsa rules supreme, Krishna is there as an antidote. This is how the rhythm of ups and downs is maintained.

The controlling force of all these events is the same, it never changes. It cannot be that there is one God in one age and another in another age.

Just a single quality gives birth to the glow of the expanded universe; in the absence of that one quality, all is pure silence. When this one single quality is known and befriended, the heart mingles with the Heart; there is that supreme sense of inalienable mutuality of oneness of quality in all, and all as belonging to the One. The supreme unity is realized; hence it is called the Supreme Self.

All time, all space and all cause have become one for eternity, the One alone is all-active. It has no gain nor loss nor death. It is unborn, eternal, and yet is born every moment and manifests itself in every epoch. All spiritual and intellectual knowledge comes to rest here.

17. THE GAYATRI HYMN

"The Hymn of hymns, oh Uddhava, is the Gayatri hymn. I shall explain it to thee from the beginning to end; pray hear." (Ekanathi Bhagawata XXI).

The Lord says, "Oh Uddhava, Gayatri hymn is the bedrock of all hymns." All means many. That in virtue of which this number comes to be experienced is Gayatri. The trisyllabic A+U+M means Omkar – The Logos. The next step starts with two numbers. The first one is the consciousness of one's own being. It is the natural characteristic, the unuttered word. It is the unknowingly spoken word given out everywhere and every moment and no one knows about it. This word, uttered unawares, is the Gayatri hymn, the basis of all hymns. Innumerable words are spoken subsequently; and all the universes spring from them, but the prime source of all is the Gayatri Chhandas, the unspoken word, the unuttered sound. Everyone has the same experience, and what is the experience born of this unspoken word? One's own being.

There are innumerable varieties of being from the ant to the gods, but what is the original being? It is Gayatri. The experience of this being is one's own being. This Gayatri

Chhandas comes first, the rest only follows. The characteristic of that being is explained by the Lord as follows: "What is the nature of that hymn? Even though there be the power to create innumerable universes, it cannot be left hold of." The original sound of the unasked for, unspoken, unthought of and unuttered word was born in the form of Chakrapani and it is unique to him; but not recognizing it, the Perfect has come to be a deplorable creature through graded degeneration in the course of the temporal process.

The pursuit of the Chhandas is fascinating. For everyone, it is the same awareness of being, the unspoken word, yet spoken. In spite of the efforts of the four Vedas, six Shastras and eighteen Puranas, its interpretation remains incomplete. Still there is the uninterrupted fascination for the Gayatri Chhandas.

What does Gayatri Chhandas mean? It is the awareness of your own being, it is whatever you understand without speech. Wherever there is life, there is the hymn to support it. It vibrates in us, and in spite of years of miserable drudgery, we do not feel like parting with it. In virtue of this Gayatri hymn Sri Rama and Sri Vishnu came to this earth as incarnations, but they mastered it. This unwitting consciousness of your own being is the same in us and in them, but they did it consciously and experienced it as such. Other beings get only to the surface of the meaning, which is only a perversion thereof; the yawning of the creatures lets out the syllables A+U+M.

Meditate on the meaning as you have understood above. You are Chakrapani, the being with a thousand hands and heads, the unuttered sound. The word and its resounding sense are the first Person, and are experienced as such. The sign of the experience is complete satisfaction of the mind. Gayatri hymn is the substratum of the satisfaction of all and it bursts forth spontaneously, for the sound is ever glorious. The name that resounds in you without being uttered is your own indwelling spirit.

It is enough if you silently listen to the ten sounds, five resoundings, dual reverberation and the single voice, and the symphony of them all. This basic Gayatri hymn is with you only.

18. SELF KNOWLEDGE AND SELF REALIZATION

Three groups of eight syllables make one series of twenty-four sounds. Gayatri

Mantra consists of twenty-four syllables as follows: Oam, Bhooh, Oam, Bhuvah, Oam, Swaha, Oam, Mahah, Oam, Janah, Oam, Tapah, Oam, Satyam, Tat, Savituih, Varenyam, Bhargah, Devasya, Dhimahi, Dhiyo, Yo, Nah, Prachodayaat. Great Rishis and Saints acquire immense power by reciting this hymn of twenty-four syllables. Innumerable worlds are created and destroyed by its power, but consider the power of the bisyllabic word Rama that easily cancels all this power and rests in perfection.

VEDAS AS BASIC: They were basic to the subsequent interpretation, hence they are called basic, but the primal root, first cause of everything is this hymn.

THE BEATITUDE OF BRAHMAN: The experience of one's own being, of the vision of one's own Self and the eventual peace that is unparalleled is called Brahmananda. The experience of one's own nature without the help of others is later on interpreted as the Great Beatitude, (Paramananda).

SPIRITUAL LIFE: Just as there is the luster of luster, so also is Gayatri Chhandas the very life of spirit. The Lord says, "I am hidden and it is my treasure, but that which hides me also reveals me. How do I appear when seen? Surely as non-dual, non-different. He who listens to the vibrating hymn is hidden. With the devout recitation of this hymn everything will be distinctly clear, for it is already there; but if one wishes to realize my vision without it, he will have it, and it will be Advaita – non-dual." (The reference is to Nama yoga as an easy alternative to Dhyana or Raja Yoga.) What do the syllables of this immovable one signify? Absolute bliss of the Self, it is Sat (being), Chit (consciousness), and Ananda (beatitude). This is the essence of the Gayatri hymn. Its contemplation confers absolute bliss.

Spiritual Knowledge and the Pacification of the Desire to Know

This universe came into being through the activity of the primal atomic (atmic) consciousness. There was nothing, not even a trace of appearance before self-consciousness, and in this state there came into being the consciousness of one's own existence, the awareness of one's own being. In fact, there was no time, nor space, nor cause. The awareness has no cause for it, hence it is futile to name one. There was no time, hence it cannot be dated. There was no space, hence its location is meaningless; yet the atomic consciousness was felt as such and nothing more – why so? For there was nothing over and above it to be aware of! The awareness only of being was there. How long this state lasted, there are no means to ascertain; but the great miracle is that the self-consciousness was there; with it was the cosmic will, followed by its realization. The atomic consciousness, on account of its will and its instant realization, became many and pervasive. Although apparently many, it is all one in essence.

When the atomic consciousness became many and pervasive on account of its will and its instantaneous realization, the energy of the single atom diversified itself into many centers, each with its own peculiarity and will; hence the conflict. At any given moment, the innumerable centers express their will in a variety of ways; generally, the willing atom does not know the "whither" and "what" of its will, but the effect is bound to be there. The tangible result of the wills of the willing atoms is to be witnessed at the moment of cosmic destruction, when the whole universe is reduced to ashes. The loving wills are not cancelled altogether; the great moments of happiness in the world are the result of these wills. The characteristic of the individual energy to will is always operative. It is its essence and it owes it to the primordial energy.

The primal energy that scintillated first is one and homogenous, but appears to be heterogeneous due to ignorance.

The quivering atomic energy is designated as the Great Principle by the Vedantas: the essential characteristic of the Principle is consciousness. The felt awareness expands itself into ether, the expanse of the ether is the space. With a single quality this Great Principle became time, space and cause. Next came the three gunas and the five elements. The speed was simply immeasurable.

The original scintillation moved in space and that was the air, the air gathered momentum and fire came into existence. The throbbing of the fire increased and became cold and that was water; the water cooled even more and that was earth. All the characteristics of the previous forms are crystallized in the earth and vibrate there; in virtue of this peculiarity there came into being innumerable varieties of living beings and vegetation, and the original quiver pulsates in and through their vital sap. The original will pervades the whole range of moving and immovable things and is constantly active there.

The scintillating characteristic prior to ether is filling every electron and proton and is constantly increasing in strength. As long as the quiver in the atoms is operative, so long the constituents must be in motion. The original will pervades the whole range of moving and immovable beings and is constantly active there.

The original consciousness sees nothing except itself. It has no organs, yet it is in action with innumerable Spiritual Knowledge and the Pacification of the Desire to Know 131 organs. It is never polluted. The various conscious centers hedged by the limiting adjuncts only think they are different from the original source, but there is only one being, one spirit, one quality; formless, timeless, non-spatial, the one, pure consciousness. There is no scope for difference or distinction. The creature, deluded by the narrow interests of "I" and "mine", suffers pain for nothing, it is limited only to itself. Everything takes place at the proper moment, in accordance with the law that binds all, and everything materializes at the proper moment. When Ravana becomes unbearable Rama is there to give relief. When Kamsa rules supreme, Krishna is there as an antidote. This is how the rhythm of ups and downs is maintained.

The controlling force of all these events is the same, it never changes. It cannot be that there is one God in one age and another in another age.

Just a single quality gives birth to the glow of the expanded universe; in the absence of that one quality, all is pure silence. When this one single quality is known and befriended, the heart mingles with the Heart; there is that supreme sense of inalienable mutuality of oneness of quality in all, and all as belonging to the One. The supreme unity is realized; hence it is called the Supreme Self.

All time, all space and all cause have become one for eternity, the One alone is all-active. It has no gain nor loss nor death. It is unborn, eternal, and yet is born every moment and manifests itself in every epoch. All spiritual and intellectual knowledge comes to rest here.

Tying It All Together

"There is happiness and unhappiness in this world only because this consciousness of I am. This consciousness of I am is the world. With the touch of this I am consciousness, this world comes into existence. Without the I am consciousness you are untouched or absolutely pure. This consciousness of I am, there is no reason or cause for it, it has just simply appeared. It comes and goes. It is impermanent. So how did I come to call myself or know myself as Siddha or accomplished? It is because of my knowledge or firm conviction that everything exists because of me, everything including this world depends on me, and not vice-versa.

I say, have respect for the Guru or God. And who is the Guru or God? The I am consciousness in its pristine purity is the Guru or God - Once you have respect for this, it will reveal all the necessary knowledge to you and you will then understand that You are beyond this "I" consciousness. You have to suffer and enjoy the consequences of this I am consciousness, there is no choice to it at all. Whatever I did not have before the birth of the I am consciousness is going to go away at death. In truth, the I am consciousness was never there, so when it goes away what do I lose? Do I die, or do I remain what I ever have been? There in That state, there is no "God" - no sense of separateness at all, no I am.

Without the intellect you know, or you are, the true state. But as soon as the intellect comes into play it is the operation of the I am consciousness. My true state is always without this I am consciousness - so if you live with this Knowledge, you won't be always thinking about death and contemplating death, and hence you will live longer physically as your mind and body will be free of unnecessary tensions, thoughts and beliefs. To understand this knowledge you need only a very pure and simple faith. I am not the result of any union between human beings, my true state is not born at all, for how can Truth or Reality change or undergo birth and death? If it does, it cannot be Truth. How to use this power of discrimination?

Lord Krishna said these same things 5000 years ago. Where is Lord Krishna now? And what happened to that time 5000 years ago? Where is it? It has gone, it has vanished, so why bother about all this, what the Scriptures have said, etc. Your true state is beyond this. Unless the knowledge of I am or Guru's grace blesses you, you will not be able to comprehend your true nature.

Even this I am consciousness does not really need anything. Your true state is beyond this I am and it has no needs, no requirements at all. In the time of Krishna there were also good people and bad people just as there are today, now they have gone. Where have they gone? Where did they come from in the first place? In truth there was no cause for their appearance, and if there is no cause there is no effect also. They have never existed in reality at all, they were only an appearance on the Reality. Existence itself is only an imagination - similarly with al of you here now listening to me. You should use this power of discrimination always, and find out in truth whether you really are a person. If you truly inquire you will find that you were never a person at all. Even the "Great Cause" or Creator finally is only a word. The "Great Cause" is the I am consciousness.

When you are an individual you have certain needs, but when you merge into the Self you no longer have these desires. When man becomes a jnani he loses all sense of being an individual and he moves about freely without any hopes or fears, he becomes completely fearless and without any desires. It is not the ears that hear or the eyes that see; the body by itself is insentient, it is the Self within that gives the feeling of being alive to the body. The body is only the instrument of the Self, it is not the Self. So long as you have the body consciousness or idea you will be subject to happiness and unhappiness, but if the body idea leaves you, even now while you are in the body, the happiness and unhappiness will also go, and you will be left with your true nature which is at all times complete and has no needs. For the realized man there is no such thing as body, mind, intellect, etc., for all these are only ideas. I don't even have the idea that by giving this knowledge I am doing good to the world. No such ideas of good and bad; no such distinctions and motives are with me. I am completely free of all false notions and ideas. That we are acting and talking here is only because of our consciousness of I am. This consciousness of I am is illusory and completely unreal to the jnani. Ultimately, until you can leave off completely the feeling of personality, you will not be able to fully comprehend the Absolute Reality. You are bound by this sense of being a person, even though this thread of a personality may be very thin, however, even then this bondage of personality is ultimately illusory.

All I am doing here is waking you up, calling "wake up, you have been dreaming!" That you are awake and are a person in a world - when you have any sense of personality like this, you are quite obviously fast asleep and dreaming although you falsely feel that you are awake. True awakening is to awaken to Reality and to know that you are not a person, and never have been a person. A person has needs and desires, but the Reality needs nothing at all, for this is your true state. It is not because I tell you, that you are the Reality. Even if I don't tell you, still you are the Reality. It is there with you at all times, a self evident fact. Whatever powers or Siddhis come to you from this knowledge, don't become involved with them, negate them immediately and remain merged in your true nature. Do whatever you want in this world, but don't lose your Identity - that is that you have no identity at all.

So with this knowledge, when I die, what happens? What I never really had goes away, what was never mine leaves me, so what have I lost? What really happens to me with the physical death? Nothing at all! Do anything you want to in this world, but be with your Self, your True nature, don't forget It, be with It, dwell with It. It is bliss Itself, it is not the nature of bliss.

I have been talking and discussing so many things here, and if you feel that you still have to go and get spiritual advice or instruction from some other teacher, then you have not understood anything that I have said here. Do not unnecessarily run after or make friends with outside things or persons, but rather remain with your own Self, nature or Reality. The idea of birth and death is nothing more than a drama or play, it has no basis in Truth, don't bother about it - it is illusory, all these ideas are illusory!"

Made in United States
Troutdale, OR
04/25/2024

19404494R00131